Mitch Albom writes for the *Detroit Free Press*, and has been voted America's No. 1 sport's columnist ten times by the Associated Press Sports Editors. Albom, a former professional musician, hosts a daily radio show on WJR in Detroit and appears regularly on ESPN's "The Sports Reporters." He is the author of *Bo* and *Fab Five*, both US bestsellers, and has also published four collections of his columns. He lives with his wife, Janine, in Michigan.

Tuesdays with Morrie

An old man, a young man,
and
life's greatest lesson

MITCH ALBOM

WARNER BOOKS

A *Warner* Book

First published in the United States in 1997
by Doubleday, a division of
Bantam Doubleday Dell Publishing Group, Inc.
First published in Great Britain in 1998
by Little, Brown and Company
Reprinted 1999 (four times), 2000 (three times), 2001

A CIP catalogue record for this book is available from the British Library.

ISBN 0 7515 2737 8

Printed and bound in Great Britain by Clays Ltd, St Ives plc

Warner Books
A Division of
Little, Brown and Company (UK)
Brettenham House
Lancaster Place
London WC2E 7EN

www.littlebrown.co.uk

THIS BOOK IS DEDICATED
TO MY BROTHER, PETER,
THE BRAVEST PERSON I KNOW.

Contents

Acknowledgments

I would like to acknowledge the enormous help given to me in creating this book. For their memories, their patience, and their guidance, I wish to thank Charlotte, Rob, and Jonathan Schwartz, Maurie Stein, Charlie Derber, Gordie Fellman, David Schwartz, Rabbi Al Axelrad, and the multitude of Morrie's friends and colleagues. Also, special thanks to Bill Thomas, my editor, for handling this project with just the right touch. And, as always, my appreciation to David Black, who often believes in me more than I do myself.

Mostly, my thanks to Morrie, for wanting to do this last thesis together. Have you ever had a teacher like this?

Tuesdays
with Morrie

The Curriculum

～～❀ The last class of my old professor's life took place once a week in his house, by a window in the study where he could watch a small hibiscus plant shed its pink leaves. The class met on Tuesdays. It began after breakfast. The subject was The Meaning of Life. It was taught from experience.

No grades were given, but there were oral exams each week. You were expected to respond to questions, and you were expected to pose questions of your own. You were also required to perform physical tasks now and then, such as lifting the professor's head to a comfortable spot on the pillow or placing his glasses on the bridge of his nose. Kissing him good-bye earned you extra credit.

No books were required, yet many topics were covered, including love, work, community, family, aging, forgiveness, and, finally, death. The last lecture was brief, only a few words.

A funeral was held in lieu of graduation.

Although no final exam was given, you were expected to produce one long paper on what was learned. That paper is presented here.

The last class of my old professor's life had only one student.

I was the student.

It is the late spring of 1979, a hot, sticky Saturday afternoon. Hundreds of us sit together, side by side, in rows of wooden folding chairs on the main campus lawn. We wear blue nylon robes. We listen impatiently to long speeches. When the ceremony is over, we throw our caps in the air, and we are officially graduated from college, the senior class of Brandeis University in the city of Waltham, Massachusetts. For many of us, the curtain has just come down on childhood.

Afterward, I find Morrie Schwartz, my favorite professor, and introduce him to my parents. He is a small man who takes small steps, as if a strong wind could, at any time, whisk him up into the clouds. In his graduation day robe, he looks like a cross between a biblical prophet and a Christmas elf. He has sparkling blue-green eyes, thinning silver hair that spills onto his forehead, big ears, a triangular nose, and tufts of graying eyebrows. Al-

though his teeth are crooked and his lower ones are slanted back—as if someone had once punched them in—when he smiles it's as if you'd just told him the first joke on earth.

He tells my parents how I took every class he taught. He tells them, "You have a special boy here." Embarrassed, I look at my feet. Before we leave, I hand my professor a present, a tan briefcase with his initials on the front. I bought this the day before at a shopping mall. I didn't want to forget him. Maybe I didn't want him to forget me.

"Mitch, you are one of the good ones," he says, admiring the briefcase. Then he hugs me. I feel his thin arms around my back. I am taller than he is, and when he holds me, I feel awkward, older, as if I were the parent and he were the child.

He asks if I will stay in touch, and without hesitation I say, "Of course."

When he steps back, I see that he is crying.

The Syllabus

His death sentence came in the summer of 1994. Looking back, Morrie knew something bad was coming long before that. He knew it the day he gave up dancing.

He had always been a dancer, my old professor. The music didn't matter. Rock and roll, big band, the blues. He loved them all. He would close his eyes and with a blissful smile begin to move to his own sense of rhythm. It wasn't always pretty. But then, he didn't worry about a partner. Morrie danced by himself.

He used to go to this church in Harvard Square every Wednesday night for something called "Dance Free." They had flashing lights and booming speakers and Morrie would wander in among the mostly student crowd, wearing a white T-shirt and black sweatpants and a towel around his neck, and whatever music was playing, that's the music to which he danced. He'd do the lindy to Jimi Hendrix. He twisted and twirled, he waved his arms like a conductor on amphetamines, until sweat was dripping down the middle of his back. No one there knew he was a prominent doctor of sociology, with years of experience as a college professor and several well-respected books. They just thought he was some old nut.

Once, he brought a tango tape and got them to play it over the speakers. Then he commandeered the floor, shooting back and forth like some hot Latin lover. When he finished, everyone applauded. He could have stayed in that moment forever.

But then the dancing stopped.

He developed asthma in his sixties. His breathing became labored. One day he was walking along the Charles River, and a cold burst of wind left him choking for air. He was rushed to the hospital and injected with Adrenalin.

A few years later, he began to have trouble walking. At a birthday party for a friend, he stumbled inexplicably. Another night, he fell down the steps of a theater, startling a small crowd of people.

"Give him air!" someone yelled.

He was in his seventies by this point, so they whispered "old age" and helped him to his feet. But Morrie, who was always more in touch with his insides than the rest of us, knew something else was wrong. This was more than old age. He was weary all the time. He had trouble sleeping. He dreamt he was dying.

He began to see doctors. Lots of them. They tested his blood. They tested his urine. They put a scope up his rear end and looked inside his intestines. Finally, when nothing could be found, one doctor ordered a muscle biopsy, taking a small piece out of Morrie's calf. The lab report came back suggesting a neurological problem, and Morrie was brought in for yet another series of tests. In one of those tests, he sat in a special seat as they zapped him with electrical current—an electric chair, of sorts—and studied his neurological responses.

"We need to check this further," the doctors said, looking over his results.

"Why?" Morrie asked. "What is it?"

"We're not sure. Your times are slow."

His times were slow? What did that mean?

Finally, on a hot, humid day in August 1994, Morrie and his wife, Charlotte, went to the neurologist's office, and he asked them to sit before he broke the news: Morrie had amyotrophic lateral sclerosis (ALS), Lou Gehrig's disease, a brutal, unforgiving illness of the neurological system.

There was no known cure.

"How did I get it?" Morrie asked.

Nobody knew.

"Is it terminal?"

Yes.

"So I'm going to die?"

Yes, you are, the doctor said. I'm very sorry.

He sat with Morrie and Charlotte for nearly two hours, patiently answering their questions. When they left, the doctor gave them some information on ALS, little pamphlets, as if they were opening a bank account. Outside, the sun was shining and people were going about their business. A woman ran to put money in the parking meter. Another carried groceries. Charlotte had a million thoughts running through her mind: *How much time do we have left? How will we manage? How will we pay the bills?*

My old professor, meanwhile, was stunned by the normalcy of the day around him. *Shouldn't the world stop? Don't they know what has happened to me?*

But the world did not stop, it took no notice at all, and as Morrie pulled weakly on the car door, he felt as if he were dropping into a hole.

Now what? he thought.

As my old professor searched for answers, the disease took him over, day by day, week by week. He backed the car out of the garage one morning and could barely push the brakes. That was the end of his driving.

He kept tripping, so he purchased a cane. That was the end of his walking free.

He went for his regular swim at the YMCA, but found he could no longer undress himself. So he hired his first home care worker—a theology student named Tony—who helped him in and out of the pool, and in and out of his bathing suit. In the locker room, the other swimmers pretended not to stare. They stared anyhow. That was the end of his privacy.

In the fall of 1994, Morrie came to the hilly Brandeis campus to teach his final college course. He could have skipped this, of course. The university would have understood. Why suffer in front of so many people? Stay at home. Get your affairs in order. But the idea of quitting did not occur to Morrie.

Instead, he hobbled into the classroom, his home for more than thirty years. Because of the cane, he took a while to reach the chair. Finally, he sat down, dropped his glasses off his nose, and looked out at the young faces who stared back in silence.

"My friends, I assume you are all here for the Social Psychology class. I have been teaching this course for twenty years, and this is the first time I can say there is a risk in taking it, because I have a fatal illness. I may not live to finish the semester.

"If you feel this is a problem, I understand if you wish to drop the course."

He smiled.

And that was the end of his secret.

ALS is like a lit candle: it melts your nerves and leaves your body a pile of wax. Often, it begins with the legs and works its way up. You lose control of your thigh muscles, so that you cannot support yourself standing. You lose control of your trunk muscles, so that you cannot sit up straight. By the end, if you are still alive, you are breathing through a tube in a hole in your throat, while your soul, perfectly awake, is imprisoned inside a limp husk, perhaps able to blink, or cluck a tongue, like something from a science fiction movie, the man frozen inside his own flesh. This takes no more than five years from the day you contract the disease.

Morrie's doctors guessed he had two years left.

Morrie knew it was less.

But my old professor had made a profound decision, one he began to construct the day he came out of the doctor's office with a sword hanging over his head. *Do I wither up and disappear, or do I make the best of my time left?* he had asked himself.

He would not wither. He would not be ashamed of dying.

Instead, he would make death his final project, the center point of his days. Since everyone was going to die, he could be of great value, right? He could be research. A human textbook. *Study me in my slow and patient demise. Watch what happens to me. Learn with me.*

Morrie would walk that final bridge between life and death, and narrate the trip.

~~~~~ The fall semester passed quickly. The pills increased. Therapy became a regular routine. Nurses came to his house to work with Morrie's withering legs, to keep the muscles active, bending them back and forth as if pumping water from a well. Massage specialists came by once a week to try to soothe the constant, heavy stiffness he felt. He met with meditation teachers, and closed his eyes and narrowed his thoughts until his world shrunk down to a single breath, in and out, in and out.

One day, using his cane, he stepped onto the curb and fell over into the street. The cane was exchanged for a walker. As his body weakened, the back and forth to the bathroom became too exhausting, so Morrie began to urinate into a large beaker. He had to support himself as he did this, meaning someone had to hold the beaker while Morrie filled it.

Most of us would be embarrassed by all this, especially at Morrie's age. But Morrie was not like most of us. When some of his close colleagues would visit, he would say to them, "Listen, I have to pee. Would you mind helping? Are you okay with that?"

Often, to their own surprise, they were.

In fact, he entertained a growing stream of visitors. He had discussion groups about dying, what it really meant, how societies had always been afraid of it without necessarily understanding it. He told his friends that if they really wanted to help him, they would treat him not with sympathy but with visits, phone calls, a sharing of their problems—the way they had always shared their problems, because Morrie had always been a wonderful listener.

For all that was happening to him, his voice was strong and inviting, and his mind was vibrating with a million thoughts. He was intent on proving that the word "dying" was not synonymous with "useless."

The New Year came and went. Although he never said it to anyone, Morrie knew this would be the last year of his life. He was using a wheelchair now, and he was fighting time to say all the things he wanted to say to all the people he loved. When a colleague at Brandeis died suddenly of a heart attack, Morrie went to his funeral. He came home depressed.

"What a waste," he said. "All those people saying all those wonderful things, and Irv never got to hear any of it."

Morrie had a better idea. He made some calls. He chose a date. And on a cold Sunday afternoon, he was joined in his home by a small group of friends and family for a "living funeral." Each of them spoke and paid tribute to my old professor. Some cried. Some laughed. One woman read a poem:

> *"My dear and loving cousin . . .*
> *Your ageless heart*
> *as you move through time, layer on layer,*
> *tender sequoia . . ."*

Morrie cried and laughed with them. And all the heartfelt things we never get to say to those we love, Morrie said that day. His "living funeral" was a rousing success.

Only Morrie wasn't dead yet.

In fact, the most unusual part of his life was about to unfold.

The Student

〜 At this point, I should explain what had happened to me since that summer day when I last hugged my dear and wise professor, and promised to keep in touch.

I did not keep in touch.

In fact, I lost contact with most of the people I knew in college, including my beer-drinking friends and the first woman I ever woke up with in the morning. The years after graduation hardened me into someone quite different from the strutting graduate who left campus that day headed for New York City, ready to offer the world his talent.

The world, I discovered, was not all that interested. I wandered around my early twenties, paying rent and reading classifieds and wondering why the lights were not turning green for me. My dream was to be a famous musician (I played the piano), but after several years of dark, empty nightclubs, broken promises, bands that kept breaking up and producers who seemed excited about everyone but me, the dream soured. I was failing for the first time in my life.

At the same time, I had my first serious encounter

with death. My favorite uncle, my mother's brother, the man who had taught me music, taught me to drive, teased me about girls, thrown me a football—that one adult whom I targeted as a child and said, "That's who I want to be when I grow up"—died of pancreatic cancer at the age of forty-four. He was a short, handsome man with a thick mustache, and I was with him for the last year of his life, living in an apartment just below his. I watched his strong body wither, then bloat, saw him suffer, night after night, doubled over at the dinner table, pressing on his stomach, his eyes shut, his mouth contorted in pain. "Ahhhhh, God," he would moan. "Ahhhhhh, Jesus!" The rest of us—my aunt, his two young sons, me—stood there, silently, cleaning the plates, averting our eyes.

It was the most helpless I have ever felt in my life.

One night in May, my uncle and I sat on the balcony of his apartment. It was breezy and warm. He looked out toward the horizon and said, through gritted teeth, that he wouldn't be around to see his kids into the next school year. He asked if I would look after them. I told him not to talk that way. He stared at me sadly.

He died a few weeks later.

After the funeral, my life changed. I felt as if time were suddenly precious, water going down an open drain, and I could not move quickly enough. No more playing music at half-empty night clubs. No more writing songs in my apartment, songs that no one would hear. I returned to school. I earned a master's degree in journalism and took the first job offered, as a sports writer. Instead of chasing my own fame, I wrote about famous athletes chasing theirs. I worked for newspapers and freelanced for magazines. I worked at a pace that knew no hours, no limits. I would wake up in the morning, brush my teeth, and sit down at the typewriter in the same clothes I had slept in. My uncle had worked for a corporation and hated it—same thing, every day—and I was determined never to end up like him.

I bounced around from New York to Florida and eventually took a job in Detroit as a columnist for the *Detroit Free Press*. The sports appetite in that city was insatiable—they had professional teams in football, basketball, baseball, and hockey—and it matched my ambition. In a few years, I was not only penning columns, I was writing sports books, doing radio shows, and appearing regularly on TV, spouting my opinions on rich football players and hypocritical college sports programs. I was part of the media thunderstorm that now soaks our country. I was in demand.

I stopped renting. I started buying. I bought a house on a hill. I bought cars. I invested in stocks and built a portfolio. I was cranked to a fifth gear, and everything I did, I did on a deadline. I exercised like a demon. I drove my car at breakneck speed. I made more money than I had ever figured to see. I met a dark-haired woman named Janine who somehow loved me despite my schedule and the constant absences. We married after a seven-year courtship. I was back to work a week after the wedding. I told her—and myself—that we would one day start a family, something she wanted very much. But that day never came.

Instead, I buried myself in accomplishments, because with accomplishments, I believed I could control things, I could squeeze in every last piece of happiness before I got sick and died, like my uncle before me, which I figured was my natural fate.

As for Morrie? Well, I thought about him now and then, the things he had taught me about "being human" and "relating to others," but it was always in the distance, as if from another life. Over the years, I threw away any mail that came from Brandeis University, figuring they were only asking for money. So I did not know of Morrie's illness. The people who might have told me were long forgotten, their phone numbers buried in some packed-away box in the attic.

It might have stayed that way, had I not been flicking through the TV channels late one night, when something caught my ear . . .

The Audiovisual

∽ In March of 1995, a limousine carrying Ted Koppel, the host of ABC-TV's "Nightline" pulled up to the snow-covered curb outside Morrie's house in West Newton, Massachusetts.

Morrie was in a wheelchair full-time now, getting used to helpers lifting him like a heavy sack from the chair to the bed and the bed to the chair. He had begun to cough while eating, and chewing was a chore. His legs were dead; he would never walk again.

Yet he refused to be depressed. Instead, Morrie had become a lightning rod of ideas. He jotted down his thoughts on yellow pads, envelopes, folders, scrap paper. He wrote bite-sized philosophies about living with death's shadow: "Accept what you are able to do and what you are not able to do"; "Accept the past as past, without denying it or discarding it"; "Learn to forgive yourself and to forgive others"; "Don't assume that it's too late to get involved."

After a while, he had more than fifty of these "aphorisms," which he shared with his friends. One friend, a fellow Brandeis professor named Maurie Stein, was so taken with the words that he sent them to a *Boston Globe* reporter, who came out and wrote a long feature story on Morrie. The headline read:

A PROFESSOR'S FINAL COURSE: HIS OWN DEATH

The article caught the eye of a producer from the "Nightline" show, who brought it to Koppel in Washington, D.C.

"Take a look at this," the producer said.

Next thing you knew, there were cameramen in Morrie's living room and Koppel's limousine was in front of the house.

Several of Morrie's friends and family members had gathered to meet Koppel, and when the famous man entered the house, they buzzed with excitement—all except Morrie, who wheeled himself forward, raised his eyebrows, and interrupted the clamor with his high, singsong voice.

"Ted, I need to check you out before I agree to do this interview."

There was an awkward moment of silence, then the two men were ushered into the study. The door was shut.

"Man," one friend whispered outside the door, "I hope Ted goes easy on Morrie."

"I hope Morrie goes easy on *Ted*," said the other.

Inside the office, Morrie motioned for Koppel to sit down. He crossed his hands in his lap and smiled.

"Tell me something close to your heart," Morrie began.

"My heart?"

Koppel studied the old man. "All right," he said cautiously, and he spoke about his children. They were close to his heart, weren't they?

"Good," Morrie said. "Now tell me something about your faith."

Koppel was uncomfortable. "I usually don't talk about such things with people I've only known a few minutes."

"Ted, I'm dying," Morrie said, peering over his glasses. "I don't have a lot of time here."

Koppel laughed. All right. Faith. He quoted a passage from Marcus Aurelius, something he felt strongly about.

Morrie nodded.

"Now let me ask *you* something," Koppel said. "Have you ever seen my program?"

Morrie shrugged. "Twice, I think."

"Twice? That's all?"

"Don't feel bad. I've only seen 'Oprah' once."

"Well, the two times you saw my show, what did you think?"

Morrie paused. "To be honest?"

"Yes?"

"I thought you were a narcissist."

Koppel burst into laughter.

"I'm too ugly to be a narcissist," he said.

～～～ Soon the cameras were rolling in front of the living room fireplace, with Koppel in his crisp blue suit and Morrie in his shaggy gray sweater. He had refused fancy clothes or makeup for this interview. His philosophy was that death should not be embarrassing; he was not about to powder its nose.

Because Morrie sat in the wheelchair, the camera never caught his withered legs. And because he was still able to move his hands—Morrie always spoke with both hands waving—he showed great passion when explaining how you face the end of life.

"Ted," he said, "when all this started, I asked myself, 'Am I going to withdraw from the world, like most people do, or am I going to live?' I decided I'm going to live—or at least try to live—the way I want, with dignity, with courage, with humor, with composure.

"There are some mornings when I cry and cry and mourn for myself. Some mornings, I'm so angry and bitter. But it doesn't last too long. Then I get up and say, 'I want to live . . .'

"So far, I've been able to do it. Will I be able to continue? I don't know. But I'm betting on myself that I will."

Koppel seemed extremely taken with Morrie. He asked about the humility that death induced.

"Well, Fred," Morrie said accidentally, then he quickly corrected himself. "I mean Ted . . ."

"Now *that's* inducing humility," Koppel said, laughing.

The two men spoke about the afterlife. They spoke about Morrie's increasing dependency on other people. He already needed help eating and sitting and moving from place to place. What, Koppel asked, did Morrie dread the most about his slow, insidious decay?

Morrie paused. He. asked if he could say this certain thing on television.

Koppel said go ahead.

Morrie looked straight into the eyes of the most famous interviewer in America. "Well, Ted, one day soon, someone's gonna have to wipe my ass."

The program aired on a Friday night. It began with Ted Koppel from behind the desk in Washington, his voice booming with authority.

"Who is Morrie Schwartz," he said, "and why, by

the end of the night, are so many of you going to care about him?"

A thousand miles away, in my house on the hill, I was casually flipping channels. I heard these words from the TV set—"Who is Morrie Schwartz?"—and went numb.

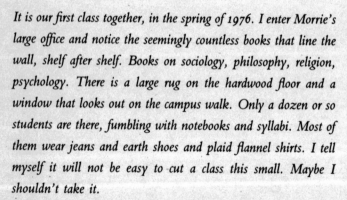

It is our first class together, in the spring of 1976. I enter Morrie's large office and notice the seemingly countless books that line the wall, shelf after shelf. Books on sociology, philosophy, religion, psychology. There is a large rug on the hardwood floor and a window that looks out on the campus walk. Only a dozen or so students are there, fumbling with notebooks and syllabi. Most of them wear jeans and earth shoes and plaid flannel shirts. I tell myself it will not be easy to cut a class this small. Maybe I shouldn't take it.

"Mitchell?" Morrie says, reading from the attendance list.

I raise a hand.

"Do you prefer Mitch? Or is Mitchell better?"

I have never been asked this by a teacher. I do a double take at this guy in his yellow turtleneck and green corduroy pants, the silver hair that falls on his forehead. He is smiling.

Mitch, I say. Mitch is what my friends called me.

"Well, Mitch it is then," Morrie says, as if closing a deal. "And, Mitch?"

Yes?

"I hope that one day you will think of me as your friend."

The Orientation

～～♪ As I turned the rental car onto Morrie's street in West Newton, a quiet suburb of Boston, I had a cup of coffee in one hand and a cellular phone between my ear and shoulder. I was talking to a TV producer about a piece we were doing. My eyes jumped from the digital clock—my return flight was in a few hours—to the mailbox numbers on the tree-lined suburban street. The car radio was on, the all-news station. This was how I operated, five things at once.

"Roll back the tape," I said to the producer. "Let me hear that part again."

"Okay," he said. "It's gonna take a second."

Suddenly, I was upon the house. I pushed the brakes, spilling coffee in my lap. As the car stopped, I caught a glimpse of a large Japanese maple tree and three figures sitting near it in the driveway, a young man and a middle-aged woman flanking a small old man in a wheelchair.

Morrie.

At the sight of my old professor, I froze.

"Hello?" the producer said in my ear. "Did I lose you? . . ."

I had not seen him in sixteen years. His hair was thinner, nearly white, and his face was gaunt. I suddenly felt unprepared for this reunion—for one thing, I was stuck on the phone—and I hoped that he hadn't noticed my arrival, so that I could drive around the block a few more times, finish my business, get mentally ready. But Morrie, this new, withered version of a man I had once known so well, was smiling at the car, hands folded in his lap, waiting for me to emerge.

"Hey?" the producer said again. "Are you there?"

For all the time we'd spent together, for all the kindness and patience Morrie had shown me when I was young, I should have dropped the phone and jumped from the car, run and held him and kissed him hello.

Instead, I killed the engine and sunk down off the seat, as if I were looking for something.

"Yeah, yeah, I'm here," I whispered, and continued my conversation with the TV producer until we were finished.

I did what I had become best at doing: I tended to my work, even while my dying professor waited on his front lawn. I am not proud of this, but that is what I did.

Now, five minutes later, Morrie was hugging me, his thinning hair rubbing against my cheek. I had told him I was searching for my keys, that's what had taken me so long in the car, and I squeezed him tighter, as if I could crush my little lie. Although the spring sunshine was warm, he wore a windbreaker and his legs were covered by a blanket. He smelled faintly sour, the way people on medication sometimes do. With his face pressed close to mine, I could hear his labored breathing in my ear.

"My old friend," he whispered, "you've come back at last."

He rocked against me, not letting go, his hands reaching up for my elbows as I bent over him. I was surprised at such affection after all these years, but then, in the stone walls I had built between my present and my past, I had forgotten how close we once were. I remembered graduation day, the briefcase, his tears at my departure, and I swallowed because I knew, deep down, that I was no longer the good, gift-bearing student he remembered.

I only hoped that, for the next few hours, I could fool him.

Inside the house, we sat at a walnut dining room table, near a window that looked out on the neighbor's house. Morrie fussed with his wheelchair, trying to get comfortable. As was his custom, he wanted to feed me, and I said all right. One of the helpers, a stout Italian woman named Connie, cut up bread and tomatoes and brought containers of chicken salad, hummus, and tabouli.

She also brought some pills. Morrie looked at them

and sighed. His eyes were more sunken than I remembered them, and his cheekbones more pronounced. This gave him a harsher, older look—until he smiled, of course, and the sagging cheeks gathered up like curtains.

"Mitch," he said softly, "you know that I'm dying."

I knew.

"All right, then." Morrie swallowed the pills, put down the paper cup, inhaled deeply, then let it out. "Shall I tell you what it's like?"

What it's like? To die?

"Yes," he said.

Although I was unaware of it, our last class had just begun.

It is my freshman year. Morrie is older than most of the teachers, and I am younger than most of the students, having left high school a year early. To compensate for my youth on campus, I wear old gray sweatshirts and box in a local gym and walk around with an unlit cigarette in my mouth, even though I do not smoke. I drive a beat-up Mercury Cougar, with the windows down and the music up. I seek my identity in toughness—but it is Morrie's softness that draws me, and because he does not look at me as a kid trying to be something more than I am, I relax.

I finish that first course with him and enroll for another. He is an easy marker; he does not much care for grades. One year, they say, during the Vietnam War, Morrie gave all his male students A's to help them keep their student deferments.

I begin to call Morrie "Coach," the way I used to address my high school track coach. Morrie likes the nickname.

"Coach," he says. "All right, I'll be your coach. And you can be my player. You can play all the lovely parts of life that I'm too old for now."

Sometimes we eat together in the cafeteria. Morrie, to my delight, is even more of a slob than I am. He talks instead of chewing, laughs with his mouth open, delivers a passionate thought through a mouthful of egg salad, the little yellow pieces spewing from his teeth.

It cracks me up. The whole time I know him, I have two overwhelming desires: to hug him and to give him a napkin.

The Classroom

∼∽ The sun beamed in through the dining room window, lighting up the hardwood floor. We had been talking there for nearly two hours. The phone rang yet again and Morrie asked his helper, Connie, to get it. She had been jotting the callers' names in Morrie's small black appointment book. Friends. Meditation teachers. A discussion group. Someone who wanted to photograph him for a magazine. It was clear I was not the only one interested in visiting my old professor—the "Nightline" appearance had made him something of a celebrity—but I was impressed with, perhaps even a bit envious of, all the friends that Morrie seemed to have. I thought about the "buddies" that circled my orbit back in college. Where had they gone?

"You know, Mitch, now that I'm dying, I've become much more interesting to people."

You were always interesting.

"Ho." Morrie smiled. "You're kind."

No, I'm not, I thought.

"Here's the thing," he said. "People see me as a

bridge. I'm not as alive as I used to be, but I'm not yet dead. I'm sort of . . . in-between."

He coughed, then regained his smile. "I'm on the last great journey here—and people want me to tell them what to pack."

The phone rang again.

"Morrie, can you talk?" Connie asked.

"I'm visiting with my old pal now," he announced. "Let them call back."

I cannot tell you why he received me so warmly. I was hardly the promising student who had left him sixteen years earlier. Had it not been for "Nightline," Morrie might have died without ever seeing me again. I had no good excuse for this, except the one that everyone these days seems to have. I had become too wrapped up in the siren song of my own life. I was busy.

What happened to me? I asked myself. Morrie's high, smoky voice took me back to my university years, when I thought rich people were evil, a shirt and tie were prison clothes, and life without freedom to get up and go—motorcycle beneath you, breeze in your face, down the streets of Paris, into the mountains of Tibet—was not a good life at all. *What happened to me?*

The eighties happened. The nineties happened. Death and sickness and getting fat and going bald happened. I traded lots of dreams for a bigger paycheck, and I never even realized I was doing it.

Yet here was Morrie talking with the wonder of our college years, as if I'd simply been on a long vacation.

"Have you found someone to share your heart with?" he asked.

"Are you giving to your community?

"Are you at peace with yourself?

"Are you trying to be as human as you can be?"

I squirmed, wanting to show I had been grappling deeply with such questions. *What happened to me?* I once promised myself I would never work for money, that I would join the Peace Corps, that I would live in beautiful, inspirational places.

Instead, I had been in Detroit for ten years now, at the same workplace, using the same bank, visiting the same barber. I was thirty-seven, more efficient than in college, tied to computers and modems and cell phones. I wrote articles about rich athletes who, for the most part, could not care less about people like me. I was no longer young for my peer group, nor did I walk around in gray sweatshirts with unlit cigarettes in my mouth. I did not have long discussions over egg salad sandwiches about the meaning of life.

My days were full, yet I remained, much of the time, unsatisfied.

What happened to me?

"Coach," I said suddenly, remembering the nick-name.

Morrie beamed. "That's me. I'm still your coach."

He laughed and resumed his eating, a meal he had started forty minutes earlier. I watched him now, his hands working gingerly, as if he were learning to use them for the very first time. He could not press down hard with a knife. His fingers shook. Each bite was a struggle; he chewed the food finely before swallowing, and sometimes it slid out the sides of his lips, so that he had to put down what he was holding to dab his face with a napkin. The skin from his wrist to his knuckles was dotted with age spots, and it was loose, like skin hanging from a chicken soup bone.

For a while, we just ate like that, a sick old man, a healthy, younger man, both absorbing the quiet of the room. I would say it was an embarrassed silence, but I seemed to be the only one embarrassed.

"Dying," Morrie suddenly said, "is only one thing to be sad over, Mitch. Living unhappily is something else. So many of the people who come to visit me are unhappy."

Why?

"Well, for one thing, the culture we have does not make people feel good about themselves. We're teaching the wrong things. And you have to be strong enough to say if the culture doesn't work, don't buy it. Create your own. Most people can't do it. They're more unhappy than me—even in my current condition.

"I may be dying, but I am surrounded by loving, caring souls. How many people can say that?"

I was astonished by his complete lack of self-pity. Morrie, who could no longer dance, swim, bathe, or walk; Morrie, who could no longer answer his own door, dry himself after a shower, or even roll over in bed. How could he be so accepting? I watched him struggle with his fork, picking at a piece of tomato, missing it the first two times—a pathetic scene, and yet I could not deny that sitting in his presence was almost magically serene, the same calm breeze that soothed me back in college.

I shot a glance at my watch—force of habit—it was getting late, and I thought about changing my plane reservation home. Then Morrie did something that haunts me to this day.

"You know how I'm going to die?" he said.

I raised my eyebrows.

"I'm going to suffocate. Yes. My lungs, because of my asthma, can't handle the disease. It's moving up my body, this ALS. It's already got my legs. Pretty soon it'll get my arms and hands. And when it hits my lungs . . ."

He shrugged his shoulders.

". . . I'm sunk."

I had no idea what to say, so I said, "Well, you know, I mean . . . you never know."

Morrie closed his eyes. "I know, Mitch. You mustn't be afraid of my dying. I've had a good life, and we all know it's going to happen. I maybe have four or five months."

Come on, I said nervously. Nobody can say—

"I can," he said softly. "There's even a little test. A doctor showed me."

A test?

"Inhale a few times."

I did as he said.

"Now, once more, but this time, when you exhale, count as many numbers as you can before you take another breath."

I quickly exhaled the numbers. "One-two-three-four-five-six-seven-eight . . ." I reached seventy before my breath was gone.

"Good," Morrie said. "You have healthy lungs. Now. Watch what I do."

He inhaled, then began his number count in a soft, wobbly voice. "One-two-three-four-five-six-seven-eight-nine-ten-eleven-twelve-thirteen-fourteen-fifteen-sixteen-seventeen-eighteen—"

He stopped, gasping for air.

"When the doctor first asked me to do this, I could reach twenty-three. Now it's eighteen."

He closed his eyes, shook his head. "My tank is almost empty."

I tapped my thighs nervously. That was enough for one afternoon.

"Come back and see your old professor," Morrie said when I hugged him good-bye.

I promised I would, and I tried not to think about the last time I promised this.

In the campus bookstore, I shop for the items on Morrie's reading list. I purchase books that I never knew existed, titles such as Youth: Identity and Crisis, I and Thou, The Divided Self.

Before college I did not know the study of human relations could be considered scholarly. Until I met Morrie, I did not believe it.

But his passion for books is real and contagious. We begin to talk seriously sometimes, after class, when the room has emptied. He asks me questions about my life, then quotes lines from Erich Fromm, Martin Buber, Erik Erikson. Often he defers to their words, footnoting his own advice, even though he obviously thought the same things himself. It is at these times that I realize he is indeed a professor, not an uncle. One afternoon, I am complaining about the confusion of my age, what is expected of me versus what I want for myself.

"Have I told you about the tension of opposites?" he says.

The tension of opposites?

"Life is a series of pulls back and forth. You want to do one thing, but you are bound to do something else. Something hurts you, yet you know it shouldn't. You take certain things for granted, even when you know you should never take anything for granted.

"A tension of opposites, like a pull on a rubber band. And most of us live somewhere in the middle."

Sounds like a wrestling match, I say.

"A wrestling match." He laughs. "Yes, you could describe life that way."

So which side wins, I ask?

"Which side wins?"

He smiles at me, the crinkled eyes, the crooked teeth.

"Love wins. Love always wins."

Taking Attendance

~~~~~ I flew to London a few weeks later. I was covering Wimbledon, the world's premier tennis competition and one of the few events I go to where the crowd never boos and no one is drunk in the parking lot. England was warm and cloudy, and each morning I walked the tree-lined streets near the tennis courts, passing teenagers cued up for leftover tickets and vendors selling strawberries and cream. Outside the gate was a newsstand that sold a half-dozen colorful British tabloids, featuring photos of topless women, paparazzi pictures of the royal family, horoscopes, sports, lottery contests, and a wee bit of actual news. Their top headline of the day was written on a small chalkboard that leaned against the latest stack of papers, and usually read something like DIANA IN ROW WITH CHARLES! or GAZZA TO TEAM: GIVE ME MILLIONS!

People scooped up these tabloids, devoured their gossip, and on previous trips to England, I had always done the same. But now, for some reason, I found myself thinking about Morrie whenever I read anything silly or mindless. I kept picturing him there, in the house with the Japanese maple and the hardwood floors, counting his breath, squeezing out every moment with his loved ones, while I spent so many hours on things that meant absolutely nothing to me personally: movie stars, supermodels, the latest noise out of Princess Di or Madonna or John F. Kennedy, Jr. In a strange way, I envied the quality of Morrie's time even as I lamented its diminishing supply. Why did we bother with all the distractions we did? Back home, the O. J. Simpson trial was in full swing, and there were people who surrendered their entire lunch hours watching it, then taped the rest so they could watch more at night. They didn't know O. J. Simpson. They didn't know anyone involved in the case. Yet they gave up days and weeks of their lives, addicted to someone else's drama.

I remembered what Morrie said during our visit: *"The culture we have does not make people feel good about themselves. And you have to be strong enough to say if the culture doesn't work, don't buy it."*

Morrie, true to these words, had developed his own culture—long before he got sick. Discussion groups, walks with friends, dancing to his music in the Harvard Square church. He started a project called Greenhouse, where poor people could receive mental health services. He read books to find new ideas for his classes, visited with colleagues, kept up with old students, wrote letters to distant friends. He took more time eating and looking at nature and wasted no time in front of TV sitcoms or

"Movies of the Week." He had created a cocoon of human activities—conversation, interaction, affection—and it filled his life like an overflowing soup bowl.

I had also developed my own culture. Work. I did four or five media jobs in England, juggling them like a clown. I spent eight hours a day on a computer, feeding my stories back to the States. Then I did TV pieces, traveling with a crew throughout parts of London. I also phoned in radio reports every morning and afternoon. This was not an abnormal load. Over the years, I had taken labor as my companion and had moved everything else to the side.

In Wimbledon, I ate meals at my little wooden work cubicle and thought nothing of it. On one particularly crazy day, a crush of reporters had tried to chase down Andre Agassi and his famous girlfriend, Brooke Shields, and I had gotten knocked over by a British photographer who barely muttered "Sorry" before sweeping past, his huge metal lenses strapped around his neck. I thought of something else Morrie had told me: *"So many people walk around with a meaningless life. They seem half-asleep, even when they're busy doing things they think are important. This is because they're chasing the wrong things. The way you get meaning into your life is to devote yourself to loving others, devote yourself to your community around you, and devote yourself to creating something that gives you purpose and meaning."*

I knew he was right.

Not that I did anything about it.

At the end of the tournament—and the countless cups of coffee I drank to get through it—I closed my computer, cleaned out my cubicle, and went back to the apartment to pack. It was late. The TV was nothing but fuzz.

I flew to Detroit, arrived late in the afternoon, dragged myself home and went to sleep. I awoke to a jolting piece of news: the unions at my newspaper had gone on strike. The place was shut down. There were picketers at the front entrance and marchers chanting up and down the street. As a member of the union, I had no choice: I was suddenly, and for the first time in my life, out of a job, out of a paycheck, and pitted against my employers. Union leaders called my home and warned me against any contact with my former editors, many of whom were my friends, telling me to hang up if they tried to call and plead their case.

"We're going to fight until we win!" the union leaders swore, sounding like soldiers.

I felt confused and depressed. Although the TV and radio work were nice supplements, the newspaper had been my lifeline, my oxygen; when I saw my stories in print in each morning, I knew that, in at least one way, I was alive.

Now it was gone. And as the strike continued—the first day, the second day, the third day—there were worried phone calls and rumors that this could go on for months. Everything I had known was upside down. There were sporting events each night that I would have gone to cover. Instead, I stayed home, watched them on TV. I had grown used to thinking readers somehow needed my column. I was stunned at how easily things went on without me.

After a week of this, I picked up the phone and dialed Morrie's number. Connie brought him to the phone.

"You're coming to visit me," he said, less a question than a statement.

Well. Could I?

"How about Tuesday?"

Tuesday would be good, I said. Tuesday would be fine.

In my sophomore year, I take two more of his courses. We go beyond the classroom, meeting now and then just to talk. I have never done this before with an adult who was not a relative, yet I feel comfortable doing it with Morrie, and he seems comfortable making the time.

"Where shall we visit today?" he asks cheerily when I enter his office.

In the spring, we sit under a tree outside the sociology building, and in the winter, we sit by his desk, me in my gray sweatshirts and Adidas sneakers, Morrie in Rockport shoes and corduroy pants. Each time we talk, he listens to me ramble, then he tries to pass on some sort of life lesson. He warns me that money is not the most important thing, contrary to the popular view on campus. He tells me I need to be "fully human." He speaks of the alienation of youth and the need for "connectedness" with the society around me. *Some of these things I under-stand, some I do not. It makes no difference. The discussions give me an excuse to talk to him, fatherly conversations I cannot have with my own father, who would like me to be a lawyer.*

Morrie hates lawyers.

"What do you want to do when you get out of college?" he asks.

I want to be a musician, I say. Piano player.

"Wonderful," he says. "But that's a hard life."

Yeah.

"A lot of sharks."

That's what I hear.

"Still," he says, "if you really want it, then you'll make your dream happen."

I want to hug him, to thank him for saying that, but I am not that open. I only nod instead.

"I'll bet you play piano with a lot of pep," he says.

I laugh. Pep?

He laughs back. "Pep. What's the matter? They don't say that anymore?"

The First Tuesday
We Talk About the World

∼∽ Connie opened the door and let me in. Morrie was in his wheelchair by the kitchen table, wearing a loose cotton shirt and even looser black sweatpants. They were loose because his legs had atrophied beyond normal clothing size—you could get two hands around his thighs and have your fingers touch. Had he been able to stand, he'd have been no more than five feet tall, and he'd probably have fit into a sixth grader's jeans.

"I got you something," I announced, holding up a brown paper bag. I had stopped on my way from the airport at a nearby supermarket and purchased some turkey, potato salad, macaroni salad, and bagels. I knew there was plenty of food at the house, but I wanted to contribute something. I was so powerless to help Morrie otherwise. And I remembered his fondness for eating.

"Ah, so much food!" he sang. "Well. Now you have to eat it with me."

We sat at the kitchen table, surrounded by wicker chairs. This time, without the need to make up sixteen years of information, we slid quickly into the familiar waters of our old college dialogue, Morrie asking questions, listening to my replies, stopping like a chef to sprinkle in something I'd forgotten or hadn't realized. He asked about the newspaper strike, and true to form, he couldn't understand why both sides didn't simply communicate with each other and solve their problems. I told him not everyone was as smart as he was.

Occasionally, he had to stop to use the bathroom, a process that took some time. Connie would wheel him to the toilet, then lift him from the chair and support him as he urinated into the beaker. Each time he came back, he looked tired.

"Do you remember when I told Ted Koppel that pretty soon someone was gonna have to wipe my ass?" he said.

I laughed. You don't forget a moment like that.

"Well, I think that day is coming. That one bothers me."

Why?

"Because it's the ultimate sign of dependency. Someone wiping your bottom. But I'm working on it. I'm trying to enjoy the process."

Enjoy it?

"Yes. After all, I get to be a baby one more time."

That's a unique way of looking at it.

"Well, I have to look at life uniquely now. Let's face it. I can't go shopping, I can't take care of the bank accounts, I can't take out the garbage. But I can sit here with my dwindling days and look at what I think is important in life. I have both the time—and the reason—to do that."

So, I said, in a reflexively cynical response, I guess the key to finding the meaning of life is to stop taking out the garbage?

He laughed, and I was relieved that he did.

As Connie took the plates away, I noticed a stack of newspapers that had obviously been read before I got there.

You bother keeping up with the news, I asked?

"Yes," Morrie said. "Do you think that's strange? Do you think because I'm dying, I shouldn't care what happens in this world?"

Maybe.

He sighed. "Maybe you're right. Maybe I shouldn't care. After all, I won't be around to see how it all turns out.

"But it's hard to explain, Mitch. Now that I'm suffering, I feel closer to people who suffer than I ever did before. The other night, on TV, I saw people in Bosnia running across the street, getting fired upon, killed, innocent victims . . . and I just started to cry. I feel their anguish as if it were my own. I don't know any of these people. But—how can I put this?—I'm almost . . . drawn to them."

His eyes got moist, and I tried to change the subject, but he dabbed his face and waved me off.

"I cry all the time now," he said. "Never mind."

Amazing, I thought. I worked in the news business. I covered stories where people died. I interviewed grieving family members. I even attended the funerals. I never cried. Morrie, for the suffering of people half a world away, was weeping. *Is this what comes at the end,* I wondered? Maybe death is the great equalizer, the one big thing that can finally make strangers shed a tear for one another.

Morrie honked loudly into the tissue. "This is okay with you, isn't it? Men crying?"

Sure, I said, too quickly.

He grinned. "Ah, Mitch, I'm gonna loosen you up. One day, I'm gonna show you it's okay to cry."

Yeah, yeah, I said.

"Yeah, yeah," he said.

We laughed because he used to say the same thing nearly twenty years earlier. Mostly on Tuesdays. In fact, Tuesday had always been our day together. Most of my courses with Morrie were on Tuesdays, he had office hours on Tuesdays, and when I wrote my senior thesis—which was pretty much Morrie's suggestion, right from the start—it was on Tuesdays that we sat together, by his desk, or in the cafeteria, or on the steps of Pearlman Hall, going over the work.

So it seemed only fitting that we were back together on a Tuesday, here in the house with the Japanese maple out front. As I readied to go, I mentioned this to Morrie.

"We're Tuesday people," he said.

Tuesday people, I repeated.

Morrie smiled.

"Mitch, you asked about caring for people I don't even know. But can I tell you the thing I'm learning most with this disease?"

What's that?

"The most important thing in life is to learn how to give out love, and to let it come in."

His voice dropped to a whisper. "Let it come in. We think we don't deserve love, we think if we let it in we'll become too soft. But a wise man named Levine said it right. He said, 'Love is the only rational act.' "

He repeated it carefully, pausing for effect. " 'Love is the only rational act.' "

I nodded, like a good student, and he exhaled weakly. I leaned over to give him a hug. And then, although it is not really like me, I kissed him on the cheek. I felt his weakened hands on my arms, the thin stubble of his whiskers brushing my face.

"So you'll come back next Tuesday?" he whispered.

He enters the classroom, sits down, doesn't say anything. He looks at us, we look at him. At first, there are a few giggles, but Morrie only shrugs, and eventually a deep silence falls and we begin to notice the smallest sounds, the radiator humming in the corner of the room, the nasal breathing of one of the fat students.

Some of us are agitated. When is he going to say something? We squirm, check our watches. A few students look out the window, trying to be above it all. This goes on a good fifteen minutes, before Morrie finally breaks in with a whisper.

"What's happening here?" he asks.

And slowly a discussion begins—as Morrie has wanted all along—about the effect of silence on human relations. Why are we embarrassed by silence? What comfort do we find in all the noise?

I am not bothered by the silence. For all the noise I make with my friends, I am still not comfortable talking about my feelings in front of others—especially not classmates. I could sit in the quiet for hours if that is what the class demanded.

On my way out, Morrie stops me. "You didn't say much today," *he remarks.*

I don't know. I just didn't have anything to add.

"I think you have a lot to add. In fact, Mitch, you remind me of someone I knew who also liked to keep things to himself when he was younger."

Who?

"Me."

The Second Tuesday
We Talk About Feeling Sorry for Yourself

~~~~ I came back the next Tuesday. And for many Tuesdays that followed. I looked forward to these visits more than one would think, considering I was flying seven hundred miles to sit alongside a dying man. But I seemed to slip into a time warp when I visited Morrie, and I liked myself better when I was there. I no longer rented a cellular phone for the rides from the airport. *Let them wait,* I told myself, mimicking Morrie.

The newspaper situation in Detroit had not improved. In fact, it had grown increasingly insane, with nasty confrontations between picketers and replacement workers, people arrested, beaten, lying in the street in front of delivery trucks.

In light of this, my visits with Morrie felt like a cleansing rinse of human kindness. We talked about life and we talked about love. We talked about one of Morrie's favorite subjects, compassion, and why our society had such a shortage of it. Before my third visit, I stopped at a market called Bread and Circus—I had seen their bags in Morrie's house and figured he must like the food there—and I loaded up with plastic containers from their fresh food take-away, things like vermicelli with vegetables and carrot soup and baklava.

When I entered Morrie's study, I lifted the bags as if I'd just robbed a bank.

"Food man!" I bellowed.

Morrie rolled his eyes and smiled.

Meanwhile, I looked for signs of the disease's progression. His fingers worked well enough to write with a pencil, or hold up his glasses, but he could not lift his arms much higher than his chest. He was spending less and less time in the kitchen or living room and more in his study, where he had a large reclining chair set up with pillows, blankets, and specially cut pieces of foam rubber that held his feet and gave support to his withered legs. He kept a bell near his side, and when his head needed adjusting or he had to "go on the commode," as he referred to it, he would shake the bell and Connie, Tony, Bertha, or Amy—his small army of home care workers—would come in. It wasn't always easy for him to lift the bell, and he got frustrated when he couldn't make it work.

I asked Morrie if he felt sorry for himself.

"Sometimes, in the mornings," he said. "That's when I mourn. I feel around my body, I move my fingers and my hands—whatever I can still move—and I mourn what I've lost. I mourn the slow, insidious way in which I'm dying. But then I stop mourning."

Just like that?

"I give myself a good cry if I need it. But then I concentrate on all the good things still in my life. On the people who are coming to see me. On the stories I'm going to hear. On you—if it's Tuesday. Because we're Tuesday people."

I grinned. Tuesday people.

"Mitch, I don't allow myself any more self-pity than that. A little each morning, a few tears, and that's all."

I thought about all the people I knew who spent many of their waking hours feeling sorry for themselves. How useful it would be to put a daily limit on self-pity. Just a few tearful minutes, then on with the day. And if Morrie could do it, with such a horrible disease . . .

"It's only horrible if you see it that way," Morrie said. "It's horrible to watch my body slowly wilt away to nothing. But it's also wonderful because of all the time I get to say good-bye."

He smiled. "Not everyone is so lucky."

I studied him in his chair, unable to stand, to wash, to pull on his pants. Lucky? Did he really say lucky?

During a break, when Morrie had to use the bathroom, I leafed through the Boston newspaper that sat near his chair. There was a story about a small timber town where two teenage girls tortured and killed a seventy-three-year-old man who had befriended them, then threw a party in his trailer home and showed off the corpse. There was another story, about the upcoming trial of a straight man who killed a gay man after the latter had gone on a TV talk show and said he had a crush on him.

I put the paper away. Morrie was rolled back in—smiling, as always—and Connie went to lift him from the wheelchair to the recliner.

You want me to do that? I asked.

There was a momentary silence, and I'm not even sure why I offered, but Morrie looked at Connie and said, "Can you show him how to do it?"

"Sure," Connie said.

Following her instructions, I leaned over, locked my forearms under Morrie's armpits, and hooked him toward me, as if lifting a large log from underneath. Then I straightened up, hoisting him as I rose. Normally, when you lift someone, you expect their arms to tighten around your grip, but Morrie could not do this. He was mostly dead weight, and I felt his head bounce softly on my shoulder and his body sag against me like a big damp loaf.

"Ahhhn," he softly groaned.

I gotcha, I gotcha, I said.

Holding him like that moved me in a way I cannot

describe, except to say I felt the seeds of death inside his shriveling frame, and as I laid him in his chair, adjusting his head on the pillows, I had the coldest realization that our time was running out.

And I had to do something.

It is my junior year, 1978, when disco and Rocky movies are the cultural rage. We are in an unusual sociology class at Brandeis, something Morrie calls "Group Process." Each week we study the ways in which the students in the group interact with one another, how they respond to anger, jealousy, attention. We are human lab rats. More often than not, someone ends up crying. I refer to it as the "touchy-feely" course. Morrie says I should be more open-minded.

On this day, Morrie says he has an exercise for us to try. We are to stand, facing away from our classmates, and fall backward, relying on another student to catch us. Most of us are uncomfortable with this, and we cannot let go for more than a few inches before stopping ourselves. We laugh in embarrassment.

Finally, one student, a thin, quiet, dark-haired girl whom I notice almost always wears bulky white fisherman sweaters, crosses her arms over her chest, closes her eyes, leans back, and does not flinch, like one of those Lipton tea commercials where the model splashes into the pool.

For a moment, I am sure she is going to thump on the floor. At the last instant, her assigned partner grabs her head and shoulders and yanks her up harshly.

"Whoa!" several students yell. Some clap.

Morrie finally smiles.

"You see," he says to the girl, "you closed your eyes. That was the difference. Sometimes you cannot believe what you see, you have to believe what you feel. And if you are ever going to have other people trust you, you must feel that you can trust them, too—even when you're in the dark. Even when you're falling."

The Third Tuesday
We Talk About Regrets

~~~ The next Tuesday, I arrived with the normal bags of food—pasta with corn, potato salad, apple cobbler—and something else: a Sony tape recorder.

I want to remember what we talk about, I told Morrie. I want to have your voice so I can listen to it . . . later.

"When I'm dead."

Don't say that.

He laughed. "Mitch, I'm going to die. And sooner, not later."

He regarded the new machine. "So big," he said. I felt intrusive, as reporters often do, and I began to think that a tape machine between two people who were supposedly friends was a foreign object, an artificial ear. With all the people clamoring for his time, perhaps I was trying to take too much away from these Tuesdays.

Listen, I said, picking up the recorder. We don't have to use this. If it makes you uncomfortable—

He stopped me, wagged a finger, then hooked his glasses off his nose, letting them dangle on the string around his neck. He looked me square in the eye. "Put it down," he said.

I put it down.

"Mitch," he continued, softly now, "you don't understand. I *want* to tell you about my life. I want to tell you before I can't tell you anymore."

His voice dropped to a whisper. "I *want* someone to hear my story. Will you?"

I nodded.

We sat quietly for a moment.

"So," he said, "is it turned on?"

~~~ Now, the truth is, that tape recorder was more than nostalgia. I was losing Morrie, we were all losing Morrie—his family, his friends, his ex-students, his fellow professors, his pals from the political discussion groups that he loved so much, his former dance partners, all of us. And I suppose tapes, like photographs and videos, are a desperate attempt to steal something from death's suitcase.

But it was also becoming clear to me—through his courage, his humor, his patience, and his openness—that Morrie was looking at life from some very different place than anyone else I knew. A healthier place. A more sensible place. *And he was about to die.*

If some mystical clarity of thought came when you

looked death in the eye, then I knew Morrie wanted to share it. And I wanted to remember it for as long as I could.

∼ The first time I saw Morrie on "Nightline," I wondered what regrets he had once he knew his death was imminent. Did he lament lost friends? Would he have done much differently? Selfishly, I wondered if I were in his shoes, would I be consumed with sad thoughts of all that I had missed? Would I regret the secrets I had kept hidden?

When I mentioned this to Morrie, he nodded. "It's what everyone worries about, isn't it? What if today were my last day on earth?" He studied my face, and perhaps he saw an ambivalence about my own choices. I had this vision of me keeling over at my desk one day, halfway through a story, my editors snatching the copy even as the medics carried my body away.

"Mitch?" Morrie said.

I shook my head and said nothing. But Morrie picked up on my hesitation.

"Mitch," he said, "the culture doesn't encourage you to think about such things until you're about to die. We're so wrapped up with egotistical things, career, family, having enough money, meeting the mortgage, getting a new car, fixing the radiator when it breaks—we're involved in trillions of little acts just to keep going. So we don't get into the habit of standing back and looking at our lives and saying, Is this all? Is this all I want? Is something missing?"

He paused.

"You need someone to probe you in that direction. It won't just happen automatically."

I knew what he was saying. We all need teachers in our lives.

And mine was sitting in front of me.

Fine, I figured. If I was to be the student, then I would be as good a student as I could be.

On the plane ride home that day, I made a small list on a yellow legal pad, issues and questions that we all grapple with, from happiness to aging to having children to death. Of course, there were a million self-help books on these subjects, and plenty of cable TV shows, and $90-per-hour consultation sessions. America had become a Persian bazaar of self-help.

But there still seemed to be no clear answers. Do you take care of others or take care of your "inner child"? Return to traditional values or reject tradition as useless? Seek success or seek simplicity? Just Say No or Just Do It?

All I knew was this: Morrie, my old professor, wasn't in the self-help business. He was standing on the tracks, listening to death's locomotive whistle, and he was very clear about the important things in life.

I wanted that clarity. Every confused and tortured soul I knew wanted that clarity.

"Ask me anything," Morrie always said.

So I wrote this list:

Death
Fear
Aging
Greed
Marriage
Family
Society
Forgiveness
A meaningful life

The list was in my bag when I returned to West Newton for the fourth time, a Tuesday in late August when the air-conditioning at the Logan Airport terminal was not working, and people fanned themselves and wiped sweat angrily from their foreheads, and every face I saw looked ready to kill somebody.

By the start of my senior year, I have taken so many sociology classes, I am only a few credits shy of a degree. Morrie suggests I try an honors thesis.

Me? I ask. What would I write about?

"What interests you?" he says.

We bat it back and forth, until we finally settle on, of all things, sports. I begin a year-long project on how football in America has become ritualistic, almost a religion, an opiate for the masses. I have no idea that this is training for my future career. I only know it gives me another once-a-week session with Morrie.

And, with his help, by spring I have a 112-page thesis, researched, footnoted, documented, and neatly bound in black leather. I show it to Morrie with the pride of a Little Leaguer rounding the bases on his first home run.

"Congratulations," Morrie says.

I grin as he leafs through it, and I glance around his office. The shelves of books, the hardwood floor, the throw rug, the couch. I think to myself that I have sat just about everywhere there is to sit in this room.

"I don't know, Mitch," Morrie muses, adjusting his glasses as he reads, "with work like this, we may have to get you back here for grad school."

Yeah, right, I say.

I snicker, but the idea is momentarily appealing. Part of me is scared of leaving school. Part of me wants to go desperately. Tension of opposites. I watch Morrie as he reads my thesis, and wonder what the big world will be like out there.

The Audiovisual, Part Two

~~~ The "Nightline" show had done a follow-up story on Morrie—partly because the reception for the first show had been so strong. This time, when the cameramen and producers came through the door, they already felt like family. And Koppel himself was noticeably warmer. There was no feeling-out process, no interview before the interview. As warm-up, Koppel and Morrie exchanged stories about their childhood backgrounds: Koppel spoke of growing up in England, and Morrie spoke of growing up in the Bronx. Morrie wore a long-sleeved blue shirt—he was almost always chilly, even when it was ninety degrees outside—but Koppel removed his jacket and did the interview in shirt and tie. It was as if Morrie were breaking him down, one layer at a time.

"You look fine," Koppel said when the tape began to roll.

"That's what everybody tells me," Morrie said.

"You sound fine."

"That's what everybody tells me."

"So how do you know things are going downhill?"

Morrie sighed. "Nobody can know it but me, Ted. But I know it."

And as he spoke, it became obvious. He was not waving his hands to make a point as freely as he had in their first conversation. He had trouble pronouncing certain words—the *l* sound seemed to get caught in his throat. In a few more months, he might no longer speak at all.

"Here's how my emotions go," Morrie told Koppel. "When I have people and friends here, I'm very up. The loving relationships maintain me.

"But there are days when I am depressed. Let me not deceive you. I see certain things going and I feel a sense of dread. What am I going to do without my hands? What happens when I can't speak? Swallowing, I don't care so much about—so they feed me through a tube, so what? But my voice? My hands? They're such an essential part of me. I talk with my voice. I gesture with my hands. This is how I give to people."

"How will you give when you can no longer speak?" Koppel asked.

Morrie shrugged. "Maybe I'll have everyone ask me yes or no questions."

It was such a simple answer that Koppel had to smile. He asked Morrie about silence. He mentioned a dear friend Morrie had, Maurie Stein, who had first sent Morrie's aphorisms to the *Boston Globe*. They had been together at Brandeis since the early sixties. Now Stein was going deaf. Koppel imagined the two men together one day, one unable to speak, the other unable to hear. What would that be like?

"We will hold hands," Morrie said. "And there'll be a lot of love passing between us. Ted, we've had thirty-five years of friendship. You don't need speech or hearing to feel that."

Before the show ended, Morrie read Koppel one of the letters he'd received. Since the first "Nightline" program, there had been a great deal of mail. One particular letter came from a schoolteacher in Pennsylvania who taught a special class of nine children; every child in the class had suffered the death of a parent.

"Here's what I sent her back," Morrie told Koppel, perching his glasses gingerly on his nose and ears. " 'Dear Barbara . . . I was very moved by your letter. I feel the work you have done with the children who have lost a parent is very important. I also lost a parent at an early age . . .' "

Suddenly, with the cameras still humming, Morrie adjusted the glasses. He stopped, bit his lip, and began to choke up. Tears fell down his nose. " 'I lost my mother when I was a child . . . and it was quite a blow to me . . . I wish I'd had a group like yours where I would have been able to talk about my sorrows. I would have joined your group because . . .' "

His voice cracked.

"'. . . because I was so lonely . . .'"

"Morrie," Koppel said, "that was seventy years ago your mother died. The pain still goes on?"

"You bet," Morrie whispered.

The Professor

〜 He was eight years old. A telegram came from the hospital, and since his father, a Russian immigrant, could not read English, Morrie had to break the news, reading his mother's death notice like a student in front of the class. "We regret to inform you . . ." he began.

On the morning of the funeral, Morrie's relatives came down the steps of his tenement building on the poor Lower East Side of Manhattan. The men wore dark suits, the women wore veils. The kids in the neighborhood were going off to school, and as they passed, Morrie looked down, ashamed that his classmates would see him this way. One of his aunts, a heavyset woman, grabbed Morrie and began to wail: "What will you do without your mother? *What will become of you?*"

Morrie burst into tears. His classmates ran away.

At the cemetery, Morrie watched as they shoveled dirt into his mother's grave. He tried to recall the tender moments they had shared when she was alive. She had operated a candy store until she got sick, after which she mostly slept or sat by the window, looking frail and weak. Sometimes she would yell out for her son to get her some medicine, and young Morrie, playing stickball in the street, would pretend he did not hear her. In his mind he believed he could make the illness go away by ignoring it.

How else can a child confront death?

Morrie's father, whom everyone called Charlie, had come to America to escape the Russian Army. He worked in the fur business, but was constantly out of a job. Uneducated and barely able to speak English, he was terribly poor, and the family was on public assistance much of the time. Their apartment was a dark, cramped, depressing place behind the candy store. They had no luxuries. No car. Sometimes, to make money, Morrie and his younger brother, David, would wash porch steps together for a nickel.

After their mother's death, the two boys were sent off to a small hotel in the Connecticut woods where several families shared a large cabin and a communal kitchen. The fresh air might be good for the children, the relatives thought. Morrie and David had never seen so much greenery, and they ran and played in the fields. One night after dinner, they went for a walk and it began to rain. Rather than come inside, they splashed around for hours.

The next morning, when they awoke, Morrie hopped out of bed.

"Come on," he said to his brother. "Get up."

"I can't."

"What do you mean?"

David's face was panicked. "I can't . . . move."

He had polio.

Of course, the rain did not cause this. But a child Morrie's age could not understand that. For a long time—as his brother was taken back and forth to a special medical home and was forced to wear braces on his legs, which left him limping—Morrie felt responsible.

So in the mornings, he went to synagogue—by himself, because his father was not a religious man—and he stood among the swaying men in their long black coats and he asked God to take care of his dead mother and his sick brother.

And in the afternoons, he stood at the bottom of the subway steps and hawked magazines, turning whatever money he made over to his family to buy food.

In the evenings, he watched his father eat in silence, hoping for—but never getting—a show of affection, communication, warmth.

At nine years old, he felt as if the weight of a mountain were on his shoulders.

~~~~> But a saving embrace came into Morrie's life the following year: his new stepmother, Eva. She was a short Romanian immigrant with plain features, curly brown hair, and the energy of two women. She had a glow that warmed the otherwise murky atmosphere his father cre-

ated. She talked when her new husband was silent, she sang songs to the children at night. Morrie took comfort in her soothing voice, her school lessons, her strong character. When his brother returned from the medical home, still wearing leg braces from the polio, the two of them shared a rollaway bed in the kitchen of their apartment, and Eva would kiss them good-night. Morrie waited on those kisses like a puppy waits on milk, and he felt, deep down, that he had a mother again.

There was no escaping their poverty, however. They lived now in the Bronx, in a one-bedroom apartment in a redbrick building on Tremont Avenue, next to an Italian beer garden where the old men played boccie on summer evenings. Because of the Depression, Morrie's father found even less work in the fur business. Sometimes when the family sat at the dinner table, all Eva could put out was bread.

"What else is there?" David would ask.

"Nothing else," she would answer.

When she tucked Morrie and David into bed, she would sing to them in Yiddish. Even the songs were sad and poor. There was one about a girl trying to sell her cigarettes:

> *Please buy my cigarettes.*
> *They are dry, not wet by rain.*
> *Take pity on me, take pity on me.*

Still, despite their circumstances, Morrie was taught to love and to care. And to learn. Eva would accept nothing less than excellence in school, because she saw education as the only antidote to their poverty. She herself went to night school to improve her English. Morrie's love for education was hatched in her arms.

He studied at night, by the lamp at the kitchen table. And in the mornings he would go to synagogue to say Yizkor—the memorial prayer for the dead—for his mother. He did this to keep her memory alive. Incredibly, Morrie had been told by his father never to talk about her. Charlie wanted young David to think Eva was his natural mother.

It was a terrible burden to Morrie. For years, the only evidence Morrie had of his mother was the telegram announcing her death. He had hidden it the day it arrived.

He would keep it the rest of his life.

When Morrie was a teenager, his father took him to a fur factory where he worked. This was during the Depression. The idea was to get Morrie a job.

He entered the factory, and immediately felt as if the walls had closed in around him. The room was dark and hot, the windows covered with filth, and the machines were packed tightly together, churning like train wheels. The fur hairs were flying, creating a thickened air, and the workers, sewing the pelts together, were bent over their needles as the boss marched up and down the rows, screaming for them to go faster. Morrie could barely breathe. He stood next to his father, frozen with fear, hoping the boss wouldn't scream at him, too.

During lunch break, his father took Morrie to the boss and pushed him in front of him, asking if there was any work for his son. But there was barely enough work for the adult laborers, and no one was giving it up.

This, for Morrie, was a blessing. He hated the place. He made another vow that he kept to the end of his life: he would never do any work that exploited someone else, and he would never allow himself to make money off the sweat of others.

"What will you do?" Eva would ask him.

"I don't know," he would say. He ruled out law, because he didn't like lawyers, and he ruled out medicine, because he couldn't take the sight of blood.

"What will you do?"

It was only through default that the best professor I ever had became a teacher.

"A teacher affects eternity; he can never tell where his influence stops."

—HENRY ADAMS

The Fourth Tuesday
We Talk About Death

〰️ "Let's begin with this idea," Morrie said. "Everyone knows they're going to die, but nobody believes it."

He was in a businesslike mood this Tuesday. The subject was death, the first item on my list. Before I arrived, Morrie had scribbled a few notes on small white pieces of paper so that he wouldn't forget. His shaky handwriting was now indecipherable to everyone but him. It was almost Labor Day, and through the office window I could see the spinach-colored hedges of the backyard and hear the yells of children playing down the street, their last week of freedom before school began.

Back in Detroit, the newspaper strikers were gearing up for a huge holiday demonstration, to show the solidarity of unions against management. On the plane ride in, I had read about a woman who had shot her husband and two daughters as they lay sleeping, claiming she was protecting them from "the bad people." In California, the lawyers in the O. J. Simpson trial were becoming huge celebrities.

Here in Morrie's office, life went on one precious day at a time. Now we sat together, a few feet from the newest addition to the house: an oxygen machine. It was small and portable, about knee-high. On some nights, when he couldn't get enough air to swallow, Morrie attached the long plastic tubing to his nose, clamping on his nostrils like a leech. I hated the idea of Morrie connected to a machine of any kind, and I tried not to look at it as Morrie spoke.

"Everyone knows they're going to die," he said again, "but nobody believes it. If we did, we would do things differently."

So we kid ourselves about death, I said.

"Yes. But there's a better approach. To know you're going to die, and to be *prepared* for it at any time. That's better. That way you can actually be *more* involved in your life while you're living."

How can you ever be prepared to die?

"Do what the Buddhists do. Every day, have a little bird on your shoulder that asks, 'Is today the day? Am I ready? Am I doing all I need to do? Am I being the person I want to be?'"

He turned his head to his shoulder as if the bird were there now.

"Is today the day I die?" he said.

Morrie borrowed freely from all religions. He was born Jewish, but became an agnostic when he was a teenager, partly because of all that had happened to him as a child. He enjoyed some of the philosophies of Buddhism and Christianity, and he still felt at home, culturally, in Judaism. He was a religious mutt, which made him even more open to the students he taught over the years. And the things he was saying in his final months on earth seemed to transcend all religious differences. Death has a way of doing that.

"The truth is, Mitch," he said, "once you learn how to die, you learn how to live."

I nodded.

"I'm going to say it again," he said. "Once you learn how to die, you learn how to live." He smiled, and I realized what he was doing. He was making sure I absorbed this point, without embarrassing me by asking. It was part of what made him a good teacher.

Did you think much about death before you got sick, I asked.

"No." Morrie smiled. "I was like everyone else. I once told a friend of mine, in a moment of exuberance, 'I'm gonna be the healthiest old man you ever met!' "

How old were you?

"In my sixties."

So you were optimistic.

"Why not? Like I said, no one really believes they're going to die."

But everyone knows someone who has died, I said. Why is it so hard to think about dying?

"Because," Morrie continued, "most of us all walk around as if we're sleepwalking. We really don't experience the world fully, because we're half-asleep, doing things we automatically think we have to do."

And facing death changes all that?

"Oh, yes. You strip away all that stuff and you focus on the essentials. When you realize you are going to die, you see everything much differently.

He sighed. "Learn how to die, and you learn how to live."

I noticed that he quivered now when he moved his hands. His glasses hung around his neck, and when he lifted them to his eyes, they slid around his temples, as if he were trying to put them on someone else in the dark. I reached over to help guide them onto his ears.

"Thank you," Morrie whispered. He smiled when my hand brushed up against his head. The slightest human contact was immediate joy.

"Mitch. Can I tell you something?"

Of course, I said.

"You might not like it."

Why not?

"Well, the truth is, if you really listen to that bird on your shoulder, *if you accept that you can die at any time—* then you might not be as ambitious as you are."

I forced a small grin.

"The things you spend so much time on—all this work you do—might not seem as important. You might have to make room for some more spiritual things."

Spiritual things?

"You hate that word, don't you? 'Spiritual.' You think it's touchy-feely stuff."

Well, I said.

He tried to wink, a bad try, and I broke down and laughed.

"Mitch," he said, laughing along, "even I don't know what 'spiritual development' really means. But I do know we're deficient in some way. We are too involved in materialistic things, and they don't satisfy us. The loving relationships we have, the universe around us, we take these things for granted."

He nodded toward the window with the sunshine streaming in. "You see that? You can go out there, outside, anytime. You can run up and down the block and go crazy. I can't do that. I can't go out. I can't run. I can't be out there without fear of getting sick. But you know what? I *appreciate* that window more than you do."

Appreciate it?

"Yes. I look out that window every day. I notice the change in the trees, how strong the wind is blowing. It's as if I can see time actually passing through that window-pane. Because I know my time is almost done, I am drawn to nature like I'm seeing it for the first time."

He stopped, and for a moment we both just looked out the window. I tried to see what he saw. I tried to see time and seasons, my life passing in slow motion. Morrie dropped his head slightly and curled it toward his shoulder.

"Is it today, little bird?" he asked. "Is it today?"

Letters from around the world kept coming to Morrie, thanks to the "Nightline" appearances. He would sit, when he was up to it, and dictate the responses to friends and family who gathered for their letter-writing sessions.

One Sunday when his sons, Rob and Jon, were home, they all gathered in the living room. Morrie sat in his wheelchair, his skinny legs under a blanket. When he got cold, one of his helpers draped a nylon jacket over his shoulders.

"What's the first letter?" Morrie said.

A colleague read a note from a woman named Nancy, who had lost her mother to ALS. She wrote to say how much she had suffered through the loss and how she knew that Morrie must be suffering, too.

"All right," Morrie said when the reading was complete. He shut his eyes. "Let's start by saying, 'Dear Nancy, you touched me very much with your story about your mother. And I understand what you went through.

There is sadness and suffering on both parts. Grieving has been good for me, and I hope it has been good for you also.' "

"You might want to change that last line," Rob said.

Morrie thought for a second, then said, "You're right. How about 'I hope you can find the healing power in grieving.' Is that better?"

Rob nodded.

"Add 'thank you, Morrie,' " Morrie said.

Another letter was read from a woman named Jane, who was thanking him for his inspiration on the "Night-line" program. She referred to him as a prophet.

"That's a very high compliment," said a colleague. "A prophet."

Morrie made a face. He obviously didn't agree with the assessment. "Let's thank her for her high praise. And tell her I'm glad my words meant something to her.

"And don't forget to sign 'Thank you, Morrie.' "

There was a letter from a man in England who had lost his mother and asked Morrie to help him contact her through the spiritual world. There was a letter from a couple who wanted to drive to Boston to meet him. There was a long letter from a former graduate student who wrote about her life after the university. It told of a murder-suicide and three stillborn births. It told of a mother who died from ALS. It expressed fear that she, the daughter, would also contract the disease. It went on and on. Two pages. Three pages. Four pages.

Morrie sat through the long, grim tale. When it was finally finished, he said softly, "Well, what do we answer?"

The group was quiet. Finally, Rob said, "How about, 'Thanks for your long letter?'"

Everyone laughed. Morrie looked at his son and beamed.

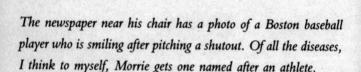

The newspaper near his chair has a photo of a Boston baseball player who is smiling after pitching a shutout. Of all the diseases, I think to myself, Morrie gets one named after an athlete.

You remember Lou Gehrig, I ask?

"I remember him in the stadium, saying good-bye."

So you remember the famous line.

"Which one?"

Come on. Lou Gehrig. "Pride of the Yankees"? The speech that echoes over the loudspeakers?

"Remind me," Morrie says. "Do the speech."

Through the open window I hear the sound of a garbage truck. Although it is hot, Morrie is wearing long sleeves, with a blanket over his legs, his skin pale. The disease owns him.

I raise my voice and do the Gehrig imitation, where the

words bounce off the stadium walls: "Too-dayyy . . . I feeel like . . . the luckiest maaaan . . . on the face of the earth . . ."

Morrie closes his eyes and nods slowly.

"Yeah. Well. I didn't say that."

The Fifth Tuesday
We Talk About Family

It was the first week in September, back-to-school week, and after thirty-five consecutive autumns, my old professor did not have a class waiting for him on a college campus. Boston was teeming with students, double-parked on side streets, unloading trunks. And here was Morrie in his study. It seemed wrong, like those football players who finally retire and have to face that first Sunday at home, watching on TV, thinking, *I could still do that*. I have learned from dealing with those players that it is best to leave them alone when their old seasons come around. Don't say anything. But then, I didn't need to remind Morrie of his dwindling time.

For our taped conversations, we had switched from handheld microphones—because it was too difficult now for Morrie to hold anything that long—to the lavaliere kind popular with TV newspeople. You can clip these onto a collar or lapel. Of course, since Morrie only wore soft cotton shirts that hung loosely on his ever-shrinking frame, the microphone sagged and flopped, and I had to reach over and adjust it frequently. Morrie seemed to enjoy this because it brought me close to him, in hugging range, and his need for physical affection was stronger than ever. When I leaned in, I heard his wheezing breath and his weak coughing, and he smacked his lips softly before he swallowed.

"Well, my friend," he said, "what are we talking about today?"

How about family?

"Family." He mulled it over for a moment. "Well, you see mine, all around me."

He nodded to photos on his bookshelves, of Morrie as a child with his grandmother; Morrie as a young man with his brother, David; Morrie with his wife, Charlotte; Morrie with his two sons, Rob, a journalist in Tokyo, and Jon, a computer expert in Boston.

"I think, in light of what we've been talking about all these weeks, family becomes even more important," he said.

"The fact is, there is no foundation, no secure ground, upon which people may stand today if it isn't the family. It's become quite clear to me as I've been sick. If you don't have the support and love and caring and concern that you get from a family, you don't have much at all. Love is so supremely important. As our great poet Auden said, 'Love each other or perish.'"

"Love each other or perish." I wrote it down. Auden said that?

"Love each other or perish," Morrie said. "It's good,

no? And it's so true. Without love, we are birds with broken wings.

"Say I was divorced, or living alone, or had no children. This disease—what I'm going through—would be so much harder. I'm not sure I could do it. Sure, people would come visit, friends, associates, but it's not the same as having someone who will not leave. It's not the same as having someone whom you know has an eye on you, is watching you the whole time.

"This is part of what a family is about, not just love, but letting others know there's someone who is watching out for them. It's what I missed so much when my mother died—what I call your 'spiritual security'—knowing that your family will be there watching out for you. Nothing else will give you that. Not money. Not fame."

He shot me a look.

"Not work," he added.

Raising a family was one of those issues on my little list—things you want to get right before it's too late. I told Morrie about my generation's dilemma with having children, how we often saw them as tying us down, making us into these "parent" things that we did not want to be. I admitted to some of these emotions myself.

Yet when I looked at Morrie, I wondered if I were in his shoes, about to die, and I had no family, no children, would the emptiness be unbearable? He had raised his two sons to be loving and caring, and like Morrie, they were not shy with their affection. Had he so desired, they would have stopped what they were doing to be with their father every minute of his final months. But that was not what he wanted.

"Do not stop your lives," he told them. "Otherwise, this disease will have ruined three of us instead of one."

In this way, even as he was dying, he showed respect for his children's worlds. Little wonder that when they sat with him, there was a waterfall of affection, lots of kisses and jokes and crouching by the side of the bed, holding hands.

"Whenever people ask me about having children or not having children, I never tell them what to do," Morrie said now, looking at a photo of his oldest son. "I simply say, 'There is no experience like having children.' That's all. There is no substitute for it. You cannot do it with a friend. You cannot do it with a lover. If you want the experience of having complete responsibility for another human being, and to learn how to love and bond in the deepest way, then you should have children."

So you would do it again? I asked.

I glanced at the photo. Rob was kissing Morrie on the forehead, and Morrie was laughing with his eyes closed.

"Would I do it again?" he said to me, looking surprised. "Mitch, I would not have missed that experience for anything. Even though . . ."

He swallowed and put the picture in his lap.

"Even though there is a painful price to pay," he said.

Because you'll be leaving them.

"Because I'll be leaving them *soon*."

He pulled his lips together, closed his eyes, and I watched the first teardrop fall down the side of his cheek.

"And now," he whispered, "you talk."

Me?

"Your family. I know about your parents. I met them, years ago, at graduation. You have a sister, too, right?"

Yes, I said.

"Older, yes?"

Older.

"And one brother, right?"

I nodded.

"Younger?"

Younger.

"Like me," Morrie said. "I have a younger brother."

Like you, I said.

"He also came to your graduation, didn't he?"

I blinked, and in my mind I saw us all there, sixteen years earlier, the hot sun, the blue robes, squinting as we put our arms around each other and posed for Instamatic photos, someone saying, "One, two, threeee . . ."

"What is it?" Morrie said, noticing my sudden quiet. "What's on your mind?"

Nothing, I said, changing the subject.

The truth is, I do indeed have a brother, a blond-haired, hazel-eyed, two-years-younger brother, who looks so unlike me or my dark-haired sister that we used to tease him by claiming strangers had left him as a baby on our doorstep. "And one day," we'd say, "they're coming back to get you." He cried when we said this, but we said it just the same.

He grew up the way many youngest children grow up, pampered, adored, and inwardly tortured. He dreamed of being an actor or a singer; he reenacted TV shows at the dinner table, playing every part, his bright smile practically jumping through his lips. I was the good student, he was the bad; I was obedient, he broke the rules; I stayed away from drugs and alcohol, he tried everything you could ingest. He moved to Europe not long after high school, preferring the more casual lifestyle he found there. Yet he remained the family favorite. When he visited home, in his wild and funny presence, I often felt stiff and conservative.

As different as we were, I reasoned that our fates would shoot in opposite directions once we hit adulthood. I was right in all ways but one. From the day my uncle died, I believed that I would suffer a similar death, an untimely disease that would take me out. So I worked at a feverish pace, and I braced myself for cancer. I could feel its breath. I knew it was coming. I waited for it the way a condemned man waits for the executioner.

And I was right. It came.

But it missed me.

It struck my brother.

The same type of cancer as my uncle. The pancreas. A rare form. And so the youngest of our family, with the blond hair and the hazel eyes, had the chemotherapy and the radiation. His hair fell out, his face went gaunt as a skeleton. *It's supposed to be me,* I thought. But my brother was not me, and he was not my uncle. He was a fighter, and had been since his youngest days, when we wrestled in the basement and he actually bit through my shoe until I screamed in pain and let him go.

And so he fought back. He battled the disease in Spain, where he lived, with the aid of an experimental drug that was not—and still is not—available in the United States. He flew all over Europe for treatments. After five years of treatment, the drug appeared to chase the cancer into remission.

That was the good news. The bad news was, my brother did not want me around—not me, nor anyone in the family. Much as we tried to call and visit, he held us at bay, insisting this fight was something he needed to do by himself. Months would pass without a word from him. Messages on his answering machine would go without reply. I was ripped with guilt for what I felt I should be doing for him and fueled with anger for his denying us the right to do it.

So once again, I dove into work. I worked because I could control it. I worked because work was sensible and responsive. And each time I would call my brother's apartment in Spain and get the answering machine—him speaking in Spanish, another sign of how far apart we had drifted—I would hang up and work some more.

Perhaps this is one reason I was drawn to Morrie. He let me be where my brother would not.

Looking back, perhaps Morrie knew this all along.

It is a winter in my childhood, on a snow-packed hill in our suburban neighborhood. My brother and I are on the sled, him on top, me on the bottom. I feel his chin on my shoulder and his feet on the backs of my knees.

The sled rumbles on icy patches beneath us. We pick up speed as we descend the hill.

"CAR!" someone yells.

We see it coming, down the street to our left. We scream and try to steer away, but the runners do not move. The driver slams his horn and hits his brakes, and we do what all kids do: we jump off. In our hooded parkas, we roll like logs down the cold, wet snow, thinking the next thing to touch us will be the hard rubber of a car tire. We are yelling "AHHHHHH" and we are tingling with fear, turning over and over, the world upside down, right side up, upside down.

And then, nothing. We stop rolling and catch our breath and wipe the dripping snow from our faces. The driver turns down the street, wagging his finger. We are safe. Our sled has thudded quietly into a snowbank, and our friends are slapping us now, saying "Cool" and "You could have died."

I grin at my brother, and we are united by childish pride. That wasn't so hard, we think, and we are ready to take on death again.

The Sixth Tuesday
We Talk About Emotions

~~~~~ I walked past the mountain laurels and the Japanese maple, up the bluestone steps of Morrie's house. The white rain gutter hung like a lid over the doorway. I rang the bell and was greeted not by Connie but by Morrie's wife, Charlotte, a beautiful gray-haired woman who spoke in a lilting voice. She was not often at home when I came by—she continued working at MIT, as Morrie wished—and I was surprised this morning to see her.

"Morrie's having a bit of a hard time today," she said. She stared over my shoulder for a moment, then moved toward the kitchen.

I'm sorry, I said.

"No, no, he'll be happy to see you," she said quickly. "I'm sure . . ."

She stopped in the middle of the sentence, turning her head slightly, listening for something. Then she continued. "I'm sure . . . he'll feel better when he knows you're here."

I lifted up the bags from the market—my normal food supply, I said jokingly—and she seemed to smile and fret at the same time.

"There's already so much food. He hasn't eaten any from last time."

This took me by surprise.

He hasn't eaten any, I asked?

She opened the refrigerator and I saw familiar containers of chicken salad, vermicelli, vegetables, stuffed squash, all things I had brought for Morrie. She opened the freezer and there was even more.

"Morrie can't eat most of this food. It's too hard for him to swallow. He has to eat soft things and liquid drinks now."

But he never said anything, I said.

Charlotte smiled. "He doesn't want to hurt your feelings."

It wouldn't have hurt my feelings. I just wanted to help in some way. I mean, I just wanted to bring him something . . .

"You *are* bringing him something. He looks forward to your visits. He talks about having to do this project with you, how he has to concentrate and put the time aside. I think it's giving him a good sense of purpose . . ."

Again, she gave that faraway look, the tuning-in-something-from-somewhere-else. I knew Morrie's nights were becoming difficult, that he didn't sleep through them, and that meant Charlotte often did not sleep through them either. Sometimes Morrie would lie awake coughing for hours—it would take that long to get the phlegm from his throat. There were health care workers now staying through the night and all those visitors during the day, former students, fellow professors, meditation teachers, tramping in and out of the house. On some days, Morrie had a half a dozen visitors, and they were often there when Charlotte returned from work. She handled it with patience, even though all these outsiders were soaking up her precious minutes with Morrie.

". . . a sense of purpose," she continued. "Yes. That's good, you know."

"I hope so," I said.

I helped put the new food inside the refrigerator. The kitchen counter had all kinds of notes, messages, information, medical instructions. The table held more pill bottles than ever—Selestone for his asthma, Ativan to help him sleep, naproxen for infections—along with a powdered milk mix and laxatives. From down the hall, we heard the sound of a door open.

"Maybe he's available now . . . let me go check."

Charlotte glanced again at my food and I felt suddenly ashamed. All these reminders of things Morrie would never enjoy.

The small horrors of his illness were growing, and when I finally sat down with Morrie, he was coughing more than usual, a dry, dusty cough that shook his chest and made his head jerk forward. After one violent surge, he stopped, closed his eyes, and took a breath. I sat quietly because I thought he was recovering from his exertion.

"Is the tape on?" he said suddenly, his eyes still closed.

Yes, yes, I quickly said, pressing down the play and record buttons.

"What I'm doing now," he continued, his eyes still closed, "is detaching myself from the experience."

Detaching yourself?

"Yes. Detaching myself. And this is important—not just for someone like me, who is dying, but for someone like you, who is perfectly healthy. Learn to detach."

He opened his eyes. He exhaled. "You know what the Buddhists say? Don't cling to things, because everything is impermanent."

But wait, I said. Aren't you always talking about experiencing life? All the good emotions, all the bad ones?

"Yes."

Well, how can you do that if you're detached?

"Ah. You're thinking, Mitch. But detachment doesn't mean you don't let the experience *penetrate* you. On the contrary, you let it penetrate you *fully*. That's how you are able to leave it."

I'm lost.

"Take any emotion—love for a woman, or grief for a

loved one, or what I'm going through, fear and pain from a deadly illness. If you hold back on the emotions—if you don't allow yourself to go all the way through them—you can never get to being detached, you're too busy being afraid. You're afraid of the pain, you're afraid of the grief. You're afraid of the vulnerability that loving entails.

"But by throwing yourself into these emotions, by allowing yourself to dive in, all the way, over your head even, you experience them fully and completely. You know what pain is. You know what love is. You know what grief is. And only then can you say, 'All right. I have experienced that emotion. I recognize that emotion. Now I need to detach from that emotion for a moment.'"

Morrie stopped and looked me over, perhaps to make sure I was getting this right.

"I know you think this is just about dying," he said, "but it's like I keep telling you. When you learn how to die, you learn how to live."

Morrie talked about his most fearful moments, when he felt his chest locked in heaving surges or when he wasn't sure where his next breath would come from. These were horrifying times, he said, and his first emotions were horror, fear, anxiety. But once he recognized the feel of those emotions, their texture, their moisture, the shiver down the back, the quick flash of heat that crosses your brain—then he was able to say, "Okay. This is fear. Step away from it. Step away."

I thought about how often this was needed in everyday life. How we feel lonely, sometimes to the point of tears, but we don't let those tears come because we are not supposed to cry. Or how we feel a surge of love for a partner but we don't say anything because we're frozen with the fear of what those words might do to the relationship.

Morrie's approach was exactly the opposite. Turn on the faucet. Wash yourself with the emotion. It won't hurt you. It will only help. If you let the fear inside, if you pull it on like a familiar shirt, then you can say to yourself, "All right, it's just fear, I don't have to let it control me. I see it for what it is."

Same for loneliness: you let go, let the tears flow, feel it completely—but eventually be able to say, "All right, that was my moment with loneliness. I'm not afraid of feeling lonely, but now I'm going to put that loneliness aside and know that there are other emotions in the world, and I'm going to experience them as well."

"Detach," Morrie said again.

He closed his eyes, then coughed.

Then he coughed again.

Then he coughed again, more loudly.

Suddenly, he was half-choking, the congestion in his

lungs seemingly teasing him, jumping halfway up, then dropping back down, stealing his breath. He was gagging, then hacking violently, and he shook his hands in front of him—with his eyes closed, shaking his hands, he appeared almost possessed—and I felt my forehead break into a sweat. I instinctively pulled him forward and slapped the back of his shoulders, and he pushed a tissue to his mouth and spit out a wad of phlegm.

The coughing stopped, and Morrie dropped back into the foam pillows and sucked in air.

"You okay? You all right?" I said, trying to hide my fear.

"I'm . . . okay," Morrie whispered, raising a shaky finger. "Just . . . wait a minute."

We sat there quietly until his breathing returned to normal. I felt the perspiration on my scalp. He asked me to close the window, the breeze was making him cold. I didn't mention that it was eighty degrees outside.

Finally, in a whisper, he said, "I know how I want to die."

I waited in silence.

"I want to die serenely. Peacefully. Not like what just happened.

"And this is where detachment comes in. If I die in the middle of a coughing spell like I just had, I need to be able to detach from the horror, I need to say, 'This is my moment.'

"I don't want to leave the world in a state of fright. I want to know what's happening, accept it, get to a peaceful place, and let go. Do you understand?"

I nodded.

Don't let go yet, I added quickly.

Morrie forced a smile. "No. Not yet. We still have work to do."

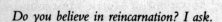

Do you believe in reincarnation? I ask.

"Perhaps."

What would you come back as?

"If I had my choice, a gazelle."

A gazelle?

"Yes. So graceful. So fast."

A gazelle?

Morrie smiles at me. "You think that's strange?"

I study his shrunken frame, the loose clothes, the socks-wrapped feet that rest stiffly on foam rubber cushions, unable to move, like a prisoner in leg irons. I picture a gazelle racing across the desert.

No, I say. I don't think that's strange at all.

The Professor, Part Two

~~~~~> The Morrie I knew, the Morrie so many others knew, would not have been the man he was without the years he spent working at a mental hospital just outside Washington, D.C., a place with the deceptively peaceful name of Chestnut Lodge. It was one of Morrie's first jobs after plowing through a master's degree and a Ph.D. from the University of Chicago. Having rejected medicine, law, and business, Morrie had decided the research world would be a place where he could contribute without exploiting others.

Morrie was given a grant to observe mental patients and record their treatments. While the idea seems common today, it was groundbreaking in the early fifties. Morrie saw patients who would scream all day. Patients who would cry all night. Patients soiling their underwear. Patients refusing to eat, having to be held down, medicated, fed intravenously.

One of the patients, a middle-aged woman, came out of her room every day and lay facedown on the tile floor, stayed there for hours, as doctors and nurses stepped around her. Morrie watched in horror. He took notes, which is what he was there to do. Every day, she did the same thing: came out in the morning, lay on the floor, stayed there until the evening, talking to no one, ignored by everyone. It saddened Morrie. He began to sit on the floor with her, even lay down alongside her, trying to draw her out of her misery. Eventually, he got her to sit up, and even to return to her room. What she mostly wanted, he learned, was the same thing many people want—someone to notice she was there.

Morrie worked at Chestnut Lodge for five years. Although it wasn't encouraged, he befriended some of the patients, including a woman who joked with him about how lucky she was to be there "because my husband is rich so he can afford it. Can you imagine if I had to be in one of those cheap mental hospitals?"

Another woman—who would spit at everyone else—took to Morrie and called him her friend. They talked each day, and the staff was at least encouraged that someone had gotten through to her. But one day she ran away, and Morrie was asked to help bring her back. They tracked her down in a nearby store, hiding in the back, and when Morrie went in, she burned an angry look at him.

"So you're one of them, too," she snarled.

"One of who?"

"My jailers."

Morrie observed that most of the patients there had

been rejected and ignored in their lives, made to feel that they didn't exist. They also missed compassion—something the staff ran out of quickly. And many of these patients were well-off, from rich families, so their wealth did not buy them happiness or contentment. It was a lesson he never forgot.

~~~~~ I used to tease Morrie that he was stuck in the sixties. He would answer that the sixties weren't so bad, compared to the times we lived in now.

He came to Brandeis after his work in the mental health field, just before the sixties began. Within a few years, the campus became a hotbed for cultural revolution. Drugs, sex, race, Vietnam protests. Abbie Hoffman attended Brandeis. So did Jerry Rubin and Angela Davis. Morrie had many of the "radical" students in his classes.

That was partly because, instead of simply teaching, the sociology faculty got involved. It was fiercely antiwar, for example. When the professors learned that students who did not maintain a certain grade point average could lose their deferments and be drafted, they decided not to give any grades. When the administration said, "If you don't give these students grades, they will all fail," Morrie had a solution: "Let's give them all A's." And they did.

Just as the sixties opened up the campus, it also opened up the staff in Morrie's department, from the jeans and sandals they now wore when working to their view of the classroom as a living, breathing place. They chose discussions over lectures, experience over theory. They sent students to the Deep South for civil rights projects and to the inner city for fieldwork. They went to Washington for protest marches, and Morrie often rode the busses with his students. On one trip, he watched with gentle amusement as women in flowing skirts and love beads put flowers in soldiers' guns, then sat on the lawn, holding hands, trying to levitate the Pentagon.

"They didn't move it," he later recalled, "but it was a nice try."

One time, a group of black students took over Ford Hall on the Brandeis campus, draping it in a banner that read MALCOLM X UNIVERSITY. Ford Hall had chemistry labs, and some administration officials worried that these radicals were making bombs in the basement. Morrie knew better. He saw right to the core of the problem, which was human beings wanting to feel that they mattered.

The standoff lasted for weeks. And it might have gone on even longer if Morrie hadn't been walking by the building when one of the protesters recognized him as a favorite teacher and yelled for him to come in through the window.

An hour later, Morrie crawled out through the window with a list of what the protesters wanted. He took the list to the university president, and the situation was diffused.

Morrie always made good peace.

At Brandeis, he taught classes about social psychology, mental illness and health, group process. They were light on what you'd now call "career skills" and heavy on "personal development."

And because of this, business and law students today might look at Morrie as foolishly naïve about his contributions. How much money did his students go on to make? How many big-time cases did they win?

Then again, how many business or law students ever visit their old professors once they leave? Morrie's students did that all the time. And in his final months, they came back to him, hundreds of them, from Boston, New York, California, London, and Switzerland; from corporate offices and inner city school programs. They called. They wrote. They drove hundreds of miles for a visit, a word, a smile.

"I've never had another teacher like you," they all said.

*As my visits with Morrie go on, I begin to read about death, how
different cultures view the final passage. There is a tribe in the
North American Arctic, for example, who believe that all things
on earth have a soul that exists in a miniature form of the body
that holds it—so that a deer has a tiny deer inside it, and a man
has a tiny man inside him. When the large being dies, that tiny
form lives on. It can slide into something being born nearby, or it
can go to a temporary resting place in the sky, in the belly of a
great feminine spirit, where it waits until the moon can send it
back to earth.*

*Sometimes, they say, the moon is so busy with the new
souls of the world that it disappears from the sky. That is why we
have moonless nights. But in the end, the moon always returns,
as do we all.*

That is what they believe.

The Seventh Tuesday
We Talk About the Fear of Aging

～ Morrie lost his battle. Someone was now wiping his behind.

He faced this with typically brave acceptance. No longer able to reach behind him when he used the commode, he informed Connie of his latest limitation.

"Would you be embarrassed to do it for me?"

She said no.

I found it typical that he asked her first.

It took some getting used to, Morrie admitted, because it was, in a way, complete surrender to the disease. The most personal and basic things had now been taken from him—going to the bathroom, wiping his nose, washing his private parts. With the exception of breathing and swallowing his food, he was dependent on others for nearly everything.

I asked Morrie how he managed to stay positive through that.

"Mitch, it's funny," he said. "I'm an independent person, so my inclination was to fight all of this—being helped from the car, having someone else dress me. I felt a little ashamed, because our culture tells us we should be ashamed if we can't wipe our own behind. But then I figured, *Forget what the culture says. I have ignored the culture much of my life. I am not going to be ashamed. What's the big deal?*

"And you know what? The strangest thing."

What's that?

"I began to *enjoy* my dependency. Now I enjoy when they turn me over on my side and rub cream on my behind so I don't get sores. Or when they wipe my brow, or they massage my legs. I revel in it. I close my eyes and soak it up. And it seems very familiar to me.

"It's like going back to being a child again. Someone to bathe you. Someone to lift you. Someone to wipe you. We all know how to be a child. It's inside all of us. For me, it's just remembering how to enjoy it.

"The truth is, when our mothers held us, rocked us, stroked our heads—none of us ever got enough of that. We all yearn in some way to return to those days when we were completely taken care of—unconditional love, unconditional attention. Most of us didn't get enough.

"I know I didn't."

I looked at Morrie and I suddenly knew why he so enjoyed my leaning over and adjusting his microphone, or fussing with the pillows, or wiping his eyes. Human touch. At seventy-eight, he was giving as an adult and taking as a child.

Later that day, we talked about aging. Or maybe I should say the fear of aging—another of the issues on my what's-bugging-my-generation list. On my ride from the Boston airport, I had counted the billboards that featured young and beautiful people. There was a handsome young man in a cowboy hat, smoking a cigarette, two beautiful young women smiling over a shampoo bottle, a sultry-looking teenager with her jeans unsnapped, and a sexy woman in a black velvet dress, next to a man in a tuxedo, the two of them snuggling a glass of scotch.

Not once did I see anyone who would pass for over thirty-five. I told Morrie I was already feeling over the hill, much as I tried desperately to stay on top of it. I worked out constantly. Watched what I ate. Checked my hairline in the mirror. I had gone from being proud to say my age—because of all I had done so young—to not bringing it up, for fear I was getting too close to forty and, therefore, professional oblivion.

Morrie had aging in better perspective.

"All this emphasis on youth—I don't buy it," he said. "Listen, I know what a misery being young can be, so don't tell me it's so great. All these kids who came to me with their struggles, their strife, their feelings of inadequacy, their sense that life was miserable, so bad they wanted to kill themselves . . .

117

"And, in addition to all the miseries, the young are not wise. They have very little understanding about life. Who wants to live every day when you don't know what's going on? When people are manipulating you, telling you to buy this perfume and you'll be beautiful, or this pair of jeans and you'll be sexy—and you believe them! It's such nonsense."

Weren't you *ever* afraid to grow old, I asked?

"Mitch, I *embrace* aging."

Embrace it?

"It's very simple. As you grow, you learn more. If you stayed at twenty-two, you'd always be as ignorant as you were at twenty-two. Aging is not just decay, you know. It's growth. It's more than the negative that you're going to die, it's also the positive that you *understand* you're going to die, and that you live a better life because of it."

Yes, I said, but if aging were so valuable, why do people always say, "Oh, if I were young again." You never hear people say, "I wish I were sixty-five."

He smiled. "You know what that reflects? Unsatisfied lives. Unfulfilled lives. Lives that haven't found meaning. Because if you've found meaning in your life, you don't want to go back. You want to go forward. You want to see more, do more. You can't wait until sixty-five.

"Listen. You should know something. All younger people should know something. If you're always battling against getting older, you're always going to be unhappy, because it will happen anyhow.

"And Mitch?"

He lowered his voice.

"The fact is, *you* are going to die eventually."

I nodded.

"It won't matter what you tell yourself."

I know.

"But hopefully," he said, "not for a long, long time."

He closed his eyes with a peaceful look, then asked me to adjust the pillows behind his head. His body needed constant adjustment to stay comfortable. It was propped in the chair with white pillows, yellow foam, and blue towels. At a quick glance, it seemed as if Morrie were being packed for shipping.

"Thank you," he whispered as I moved the pillows.

No problem, I said.

"Mitch. What are you thinking?"

I paused before answering. Okay, I said, I'm wondering how you don't envy younger, healthy people.

"Oh, I guess I do." He closed his eyes. "I envy them being able to go to the health club, or go for a swim. Or dance. Mostly for dancing. But envy comes to me, I feel it, and then I let it go. Remember what I said about detachment? Let it go. Tell yourself, 'That's envy, I'm going to separate from it now.' And walk away."

He coughed—a long, scratchy cough—and he

pushed a tissue to his mouth and spit weakly into it. Sitting there, I felt so much stronger than he, ridiculously so, as if I could lift him and toss him over my shoulder like a sack of flour. I was embarrassed by this superiority, because I did not feel superior to him in any other way.

How do you keep from envying . . .

"What?"

Me?

He smiled.

"Mitch, it is impossible for the old not to envy the young. But the issue is to accept who you are and revel in that. This is your time to be in your thirties. I had my time to be in my thirties, and now is my time to be seventy-eight.

"You have to find what's good and true and beautiful in your life as it is now. Looking back makes you competitive. And, age is not a competitive issue."

He exhaled and lowered his eyes, as if to watch his breath scatter into the air.

"The truth is, part of me is every age. I'm a three-year-old, I'm a five-year-old, I'm a thirty-seven-year-old, I'm a fifty-year-old. I've been through all of them, and I know what it's like. I delight in being a child when it's appropriate to be a child. I delight in being a wise old man when it's appropriate to be a wise old man. Think of all I can be! I am every age, up to my own. Do you understand?"

I nodded.

"How can I be envious of where you are—when I've been there myself?"

*"Fate succumbs
many a species: one alone
jeopardises itself."*

—W. H. AUDEN, MORRIE'S
FAVORITE POET

The Eighth Tuesday
We Talk About Money

I held up the newspaper so that Morrie could see it:

> I DON'T WANT MY TOMBSTONE TO READ
> "I NEVER OWNED A NETWORK."

Morrie laughed, then shook his head. The morning sun was coming through the window behind him, falling on the pink flowers of the hibiscus plant that sat on the sill. The quote was from Ted Turner, the billionaire media mogul, founder of CNN, who had been lamenting his inability to snatch up the CBS network in a corporate megadeal. I had brought the story to Morrie this morning because I wondered if Turner ever found himself in my old professor's position, his breath disappearing, his body turning to stone, his days being crossed off the calendar one by one—would he really be crying over owning a network?

"It's all part of the same problem, Mitch," Morrie said. "We put our values in the wrong things. And it leads to very disillusioned lives. I think we should talk about that."

Morrie was focused. There were good days and bad days now. He was having a good day. The night before, he had been entertained by a local a cappella group that had come to the house to perform, and he relayed the story excitedly, as if the Ink Spots themselves had dropped by for a visit. Morrie's love for music was strong even before he got sick, but now it was so intense, it moved him to tears. He would listen to opera sometimes at night, closing his eyes, riding along with the magnificent voices as they dipped and soared.

"You should have heard this group last night, Mitch. Such a sound!"

Morrie had always been taken with simple pleasures, singing, laughing, dancing. Now, more than ever, material things held little or no significance. When people die, you always hear the expression "You can't take it with you." Morrie seemed to know that a long time ago.

"We've got a form of brainwashing going on in our country," Morrie sighed. "Do you know how they brainwash people? They repeat something over and over. And that's what we do in this country. Owning things is good. More money is good. More property is good. More commercialism is good. *More is good. More is good.* We repeat it—and have it repeated to us—over and over until nobody bothers to even think otherwise. The average person is so fogged up by all this, he has no perspective on what's really important anymore.

"Wherever I went in my life, I met people wanting to gobble up something new. Gobble up a new car. Gobble up a new piece of property. Gobble up the latest toy. And then they wanted to tell you about it. 'Guess what I got? Guess what I got?'

"You know how I always interpreted that? These were people so hungry for love that they were accepting substitutes. They were embracing material things and expecting a sort of hug back. But it never works. You can't substitute material things for love or for gentleness or for tenderness or for a sense of comradeship.

"Money is not a substitute for tenderness, and power is not a substitute for tenderness. I can tell you, as I'm sitting here dying, when you most need it, neither money nor power will give you the feeling you're looking for, no matter how much of them you have."

I glanced around Morrie's study. It was the same today as it had been the first day I arrived. The books held their same places on the shelves. The papers cluttered the same old desk. The outside rooms had not been improved or upgraded. In fact, Morrie really hadn't bought anything new—except medical equipment—in a long, long time, maybe years. The day he learned that he was terminally ill was the day he lost interest in his purchasing power.

So the TV was the same old model, the car that Charlotte drove was the same old model, the dishes and the silverware and the towels—all the same. And yet the house had changed so drastically. It had filled with love and teaching and communication. It had filled with friendship and family and honesty and tears. It had filled with colleagues and students and meditation teachers and therapists and nurses and a cappella groups. It had become, in a very real way, a wealthy home, even though Morrie's bank account was rapidly depleting.

"There's a big confusion in this country over what we want versus what we need," Morrie said. "You need food, you *want* a chocolate sundae. You have to be honest with yourself. You don't *need* the latest sports car, you don't *need* the biggest house.

"The truth is, you don't get satisfaction from those things. You know what really gives you satisfaction?"

What?

"Offering others what you have to give."

You sound like a Boy Scout.

"I don't mean money, Mitch. I mean your time. Your concern. Your storytelling. It's not so hard. There's a senior center that opened near here. Dozens of elderly people come there every day. If you're a young man or young woman and you have a skill, you are asked to come and teach it. Say you know computers. You come there and teach them computers. You are very welcome there. And they are very grateful. This is how you start to get respect, by offering something that you have.

"There are plenty of places to do this. You don't need to have a big talent. There are lonely people in hospitals and shelters who only want some companionship. You play cards with a lonely older man and you find new respect for yourself, because you are needed.

"Remember what I said about finding a meaningful life? I wrote it down, but now I can recite it: Devote yourself to loving others, devote yourself to your community around you, and devote yourself to creating something that gives you purpose and meaning.

"You notice," he added, grinning, "there's nothing in there about a salary."

I jotted some of the things Morrie was saying on a yellow pad. I did this mostly because I didn't want him to see my eyes, to know what I was thinking, that I had been, for much of my life since graduation, pursuing these very things he had been railing against—bigger toys, nicer house. Because I worked among rich and famous athletes, I convinced myself that my needs were realistic, my greed inconsequential compared to theirs.

This was a smokescreen. Morrie made that obvious.

"Mitch, if you're trying to show off for people at the top, forget it. They will look down at you anyhow. And if you're trying to show off for people at the bottom, forget it. They will only envy you. Status will get you nowhere.

Only an open heart will allow you to float equally between everyone."

He paused, then looked at me. "I'm dying, right?"

Yes.

"Why do you think it's so important for me to hear other people's problems? Don't I have enough pain and suffering of my own?

"Of course I do. But giving to other people is what makes me feel alive. Not my car or my house. Not what I look like in the mirror. When I give my time, when I can make someone smile after they were feeling sad, it's as close to healthy as I ever feel.

"Do the kinds of things that come from the heart. When you do, you won't be dissatisfied, you won't be envious, you won't be longing for somebody else's things. On the contrary, you'll be overwhelmed with what comes back."

He coughed and reached for the small bell that lay on the chair. He had to poke a few times at it, and I finally picked it up and put it in his hand.

"Thank you," he whispered. He shook it weakly, trying to get Connie's attention.

"This Ted Turner guy," Morrie said, "he couldn't think of anything else for his tombstone?"

"Each night, when I go to sleep, I die. And the next morning, when I wake up, I am reborn."

—*MAHATMA GANDHI*

The Ninth Tuesday
We Talk About How Love Goes On

❧ The leaves had begun to change color, turning the ride through West Newton into a portrait of gold and rust. Back in Detroit, the labor war had stagnated, with each side accusing the other of failing to communicate. The stories on the TV news were just as depressing. In rural Kentucky, three men threw pieces of a tombstone off a bridge, smashing the windshield of a passing car, killing a teenage girl who was traveling with her family on a religious pilgrimage. In California, the O. J. Simpson trial was heading toward a conclusion, and the whole country seemed to be obsessed. Even in airports, there were hanging TV sets tuned to CNN so that you could get an O.J. update as you made your way to a gate.

I had tried calling my brother in Spain several times. I left messages saying that I really wanted to talk to him, that I had been doing a lot of thinking about us. A few weeks later, I got back a short message saying everything was okay, but he was sorry, he really didn't feel like talking about being sick.

For my old professor, it was not the talk of being sick but the being sick itself that was sinking him. Since my last visit, a nurse had inserted a catheter into his penis, which drew the urine out through a tube and into a bag that sat at the foot of his chair. His legs needed constant tending (he could still feel pain, even though he could not move them, another one of ALS's cruel little ironies), and unless his feet dangled just the right number of inches off the foam pads, it felt as if someone were poking him with a fork. In the middle of conversations, Morrie would have to ask visitors to lift his foot and move it just an inch, or to adjust his head so that it fit more easily into the palm of the colored pillows. Can you imagine being unable to move your own head?

With each visit, Morrie seemed to be melting into his chair, his spine taking on its shape. Still, every morning he insisted on being lifted from his bed and wheeled to his study, deposited there among his books and papers and the hibiscus plant on the windowsill. In typical fashion, he found something philosophical in this.

"I sum it up in my newest aphorism," he said.

Let me hear it.

"When you're in bed, you're dead."

He smiled. Only Morrie could smile at something like that.

He had been getting calls from the "Nightline" people and from Ted Koppel himself.

"They want to come and do another show with me," he said. "But they say they want to wait."

Until what? You're on your last breath?

"Maybe. Anyhow, I'm not so far away."

Don't say that.

"I'm sorry."

That bugs me, that they want to wait until you wither.

"It bugs you because you look out for me."

He smiled. "Mitch, maybe they are using me for a little drama. That's okay. Maybe I'm using them, too. They help me get my message to millions of people. I couldn't do that without them, right? So it's a compromise."

He coughed, which turned into a long-drawn-out gargle, ending with another glob into a crushed tissue.

"Anyhow," Morrie said, "I told them they better not wait too long, because my voice won't be there. Once this thing hits my lungs, talking may become impossible. I can't speak for too long without needing a rest now. I have already canceled a lot of the people who want to see me. Mitch, there are so many. But I'm too fatigued. If I can't give them the right attention, I can't help them."

I looked at the tape recorder, feeling guilty, as if I were stealing what was left of his precious speaking time. "Should we skip it?" I asked. "Will it make you too tired?"

Morrie shut his eyes and shook his head. He seemed

to be waiting for some silent pain to pass. "No," he finally said. "You and I have to go on.

"This is our last thesis together, you know."

Our last thesis.

"We want to get it right."

I thought about our first thesis together, in college. It was Morrie's idea, of course. He told me I was good enough to write an honors project—something I had never considered.

Now here we were, doing the same thing once more. Starting with an idea. Dying man talks to living man, tells him what he should know. This time, I was in less of a hurry to finish.

"Someone asked me an interesting question yesterday," Morrie said now, looking over my shoulder at the wallhanging behind me, a quilt of hopeful messages that friends had stitched for him on his seventieth birthday. Each patch on the quilt had a different message: STAY THE COURSE, THE BEST IS YET TO BE, MORRIE—ALWAYS NO. 1 IN MENTAL HEALTH!

What was the question? I asked.

"If I worried about being forgotten after I died?"

Well? Do you?

"I don't think I will be. I've got so many people who have been involved with me in close, intimate ways. And love is how you stay alive, even after you are gone."

Sounds like a song lyric—"love is how you stay alive."

Morrie chuckled. "Maybe. But, Mitch, all this talk that we're doing? Do you ever hear my voice sometimes when you're back home? When you're all alone? Maybe on the plane? Maybe in your car?"

Yes, I admitted.

"Then you will not forget me after I'm gone. Think of my voice and I'll be there."

Think of your voice.

"And if you want to cry a little, it's okay."

Morrie. He had wanted to make me cry since I was a freshman. "One of these days, I'm gonna get to you," he would say.

Yeah, yeah, I would answer.

"I decided what I wanted on my tombstone," he said.

I don't want to hear about tombstones.

"Why? They make you nervous?"

I shrugged.

"We can forget it."

No, go ahead. What did you decide?

Morrie popped his lips. "I was thinking of this: A Teacher to the Last."

He waited while I absorbed it.

A Teacher to the Last.

"Good?" he said.

Yes, I said. Very good.

I came to love the way Morrie lit up when I entered the room. He did this for many people, I know, but it was his special talent to make each visitor feel that the smile was unique.

"Ahhhh, it's my buddy," he would say when he saw me, in that foggy, high-pitched voice. And it didn't stop with the greeting. When Morrie was with you, he was really with you. He looked you straight in the eye, and he listened as if you were the only person in the world. How much better would people get along if their first encounter each day were like this—instead of a grumble from a waitress or a bus driver or a boss?

"I believe in being fully present," Morrie said. "That means you should be *with* the person you're with. When I'm talking to you now, Mitch, I try to keep focused only on what is going on between us. I am not thinking about something we said last week. I am not thinking of what's coming up this Friday. I am not thinking about doing another Koppel show, or about what medications I'm taking.

"I am talking to you. I am thinking about you."

I remembered how he used to teach this idea in the Group Process class back at Brandeis. I had scoffed back then, thinking this was hardly a lesson plan for a university course. Learning to pay attention? How important could that be? I now know it is more important than almost everything they taught us in college.

Morrie motioned for my hand, and as I gave it to him, I felt a surge of guilt. Here was a man who, if he wanted, could spend every waking moment in self-pity, feeling his body for decay, counting his breaths. So many people with far smaller problems are so self-absorbed, their eyes glaze over if you speak for more than thirty seconds. They already have something else in mind—a friend to call, a fax to send, a lover they're daydreaming about. They only snap back to full attention when you finish talking, at which point they say "Uh-huh" or "Yeah, really" and fake their way back to the moment.

"Part of the problem, Mitch, is that everyone is in such a hurry," Morrie said. "People haven't found meaning in their lives, so they're running all the time looking for it. They think the next car, the next house, the next job. Then they find those things are empty, too, and they keep running."

Once you start running, I said, it's hard to slow yourself down.

"Not so hard," he said, shaking his head. "Do you know what I do? When someone wants to get ahead of me in traffic—when I used to be able to drive—I would raise my hand . . ."

He tried to do this now, but the hand lifted weakly, only six inches.

". . . I would raise my hand, as if I was going to make a negative gesture, and then I would wave and smile. Instead of giving them the finger, you let them go, and you smile.

"You know what? A lot of times they smiled back.

"The truth is, I don't have to be in that much of a hurry with my car. I would rather put my energies into people."

He did this better than anyone I'd ever known. Those who sat with him saw his eyes go moist when they spoke about something horrible, or crinkle in delight when they told him a really bad joke. He was always ready to openly display the emotion so often missing from my baby boomer generation. We are great at small talk: "What do you do?" "Where do you live?" But *really* listening to someone—without trying to sell them something, pick them up, recruit them, or get some kind of status in return—how often do we get this anymore? I believe many visitors in the last few months of Morrie's life were drawn not because of the attention they wanted to pay to him but because of the attention he paid *to them*. Despite his personal pain and decay, this little old man listened the way they always wanted someone to listen.

I told him he was the father everyone wishes they had.

"Well," he said, closing his eyes, "I have some experience in that area . . ."

The last time Morrie saw his own father was in a city morgue. Charlie Schwartz was a quiet man who liked to read his newspaper, alone, under a streetlamp on Tremont Avenue in the Bronx. Every night, when Morrie was little, Charlie would go for a walk after dinner. He was a small Russian man, with a ruddy complexion and a full head of grayish hair. Morrie and his brother, David, would look out the window and see him leaning against the lamppost, and Morrie wished he would come inside and talk to them, but he rarely did. Nor did he tuck them in, nor kiss them good-night.

Morrie always swore he would do these things for his own children if he ever had any. And years later, when he had them, he did.

Meanwhile, as Morrie raised his own children, Charlie was still living in the Bronx. He still took that walk. He still read the paper. One night, he went outside after dinner. A few blocks from home, he was accosted by two robbers.

"Give us your money," one said, pulling a gun.

Frightened, Charlie threw down his wallet and began to run. He ran through the streets, and kept running until he reached the steps of a relative's house, where he collapsed on the porch.

Heart attack.

He died that night.

Morrie was called to identify the body. He flew to New York and went to the morgue. He was taken downstairs, to the cold room where the corpses were kept.

"Is this your father?" the attendant asked.

Morrie looked at the body behind the glass, the body of the man who had scolded him and molded him and taught him to work, who had been quiet when Morrie wanted him to speak, who had told Morrie to swallow his memories of his mother when he wanted to share them with the world.

He nodded and he walked away. The horror of the room, he would later say, sucked all other functions out of him. He did not cry until days later.

Still, his father's death helped prepare Morrie for his own. This much he knew: there would be lots of holding and kissing and talking and laughter and no good-byes left unsaid, all the things he missed with his father and his mother.

When the final moment came, Morrie wanted his loved ones around him, knowing what was happening. No one would get a phone call, or a telegram, or have to look through a glass window in some cold and foreign basement.

In the South American rainforest, there is a tribe called the Desana, who see the world as a fixed quantity of energy that flows between all creatures. Every birth must therefore engender a death, and every death bring forth another birth. This way, the energy of the world remains complete.

When they hunt for food, the Desana know that the animals they kill will leave a hole in the spiritual well. But that hole will be filled, they believe, by the souls of the Desana hunters when they die. Were there no men dying, there would be no birds or fish being born. I like this idea. Morrie likes it, too. The closer he gets to good-bye, the more he seems to feel we are all creatures in the same forest. What we take, we must replenish.

"It's only fair," he says.

The Tenth Tuesday
We Talk About Marriage

~~~~~ I brought a visitor to meet Morrie. My wife.

He had been asking me since the first day I came. "When do I meet Janine?" "When are you bringing her?" I'd always had excuses until a few days earlier, when I called his house to see how he was doing.

It took a while for Morrie to get to the receiver. And when he did, I could hear the fumbling as someone held it to his ear. He could no longer lift a phone by himself.

"Hiiiiii," he gasped.

You doing okay, Coach?

I heard him exhale. "Mitch . . . your coach . . . isn't having such a great day . . ."

His sleeping time was getting worse. He needed oxygen almost nightly now, and his coughing spells had become frightening. One cough could last an hour, and he never knew if he'd be able to stop. He always said he would die when the disease got his lungs. I shuddered when I thought how close death was.

I'll see you on Tuesday, I said. You'll have a better day then.

"Mitch."

Yeah?

"Is your wife there with you?"

She was sitting next to me.

"Put her on. I want to hear her voice."

Now, I am married to a woman blessed with far more intuitive kindness than I. Although she had never met Morrie, she took the phone—I would have shaken my head and whispered, "I'm not here! I'm not here!"—and in a minute, she was connecting with my old professor as if they'd known each other since college. I sensed this, even though all I heard on my end was "Uh-huh . . . Mitch told me . . . oh, thank you . . ."

When she hung up, she said, "I'm coming next trip."

And that was that.

Now we sat in his office, surrounding him in his recliner. Morrie, by his own admission, was a harmless flirt, and while he often had to stop for coughing, or to use the commode, he seemed to find new reserves of energy with Janine in the room. He looked at photos from our wedding, which Janine had brought along.

"You are from Detroit?" Morrie said.

Yes, Janine said.

"I taught in Detroit for one year, in the late forties. I remember a funny story about that."

He stopped to blow his nose. When he fumbled with

the tissue, I held it in place and he blew weakly into it. I squeezed it lightly against his nostrils, then pulled it off, like a mother does to a child in a car seat.

"Thank you, Mitch." He looked at Janine. "My helper, this one is."

Janine smiled.

"Anyhow. My story. There were a bunch of sociologists at the university, and we used to play poker with other staff members, including this guy who was a surgeon. One night, after the game, he said, 'Morrie, I want to come see you work.' I said fine. So he came to one of my classes and watched me teach.

"After the class was over he said, 'All right, now, how would you like to see me work? I have an operation tonight.' I wanted to return the favor, so I said okay.

"He took me up to the hospital. He said, 'Scrub down, put on a mask, and get into a gown.' And next thing I knew, I was right next to him at the operating table. There was this woman, the patient, on the table, naked from the waist down. And he took a knife and went zip—just like that! Well . . ."

Morrie lifted a finger and spun it around.

". . . I started to go like this. I'm about to faint. All the blood. Yech. The nurse next to me said, 'What's the matter, Doctor?' and I said, 'I'm no damn doctor! *Get me out of here!*'"

We laughed, and Morrie laughed, too, as hard as he could, with his limited breathing. It was the first time in weeks that I could recall him telling a story like this. How strange, I thought, that he nearly fainted once from watching someone else's illness, and now he was so able to endure his own.

Connie knocked on the door and said that Morrie's lunch was ready. It was not the carrot soup and vegetable cakes and Greek pasta I had brought that morning from Bread and Circus. Although I tried to buy the softest of foods now, they were still beyond Morrie's limited strength to chew and swallow. He was eating mostly liquid supplements, with perhaps a bran muffin tossed in until it was mushy and easily digested. Charlotte would puree almost everything in a blender now. He was taking food through a straw. I still shopped every week and walked in with bags to show him, but it was more for the look on his face than anything else. When I opened the refrigerator, I would see an overflow of containers. I guess I was hoping that one day we would go back to eating a real lunch together and I could watch the sloppy way in which he talked while chewing, the food spilling happily out of his mouth. This was a foolish hope.

"So . . . Janine," Morrie said.

She smiled.

"You are lovely. Give me your hand."

She did.

"Mitch says that you're a professional singer."

Yes, Janine said.

"He says you're great."

Oh, she laughed. No. He just says that.

Morrie raised his eyebrows. "Will you sing something for me?"

Now, I have heard people ask this of Janine for almost as long as I have known her. When people find out you sing for a living, they always say, "Sing something for us." Shy about her talent, and a perfectionist about conditions, Janine never did. She would politely decline. Which is what I expected now.

Which is when she began to sing:

"The very thought of you
and I forget to do
the little ordinary things that everyone ought to do . . ."

It was a 1930s standard, written by Ray Noble, and Janine sang it sweetly, looking straight at Morrie. I was amazed, once again, at his ability to draw emotion from people who otherwise kept it locked away. Morrie closed his eyes to absorb the notes. As my wife's loving voice filled the room, a crescent smile appeared on his face. And while his body was stiff as a sandbag, you could almost see him dancing inside it.

146

> *"I see your face in every flower,*
> *your eyes in stars above,*
> *it's just the thought of you,*
> *the very thought of you,*
> *my love . . ."*

When she finished, Morrie opened his eyes and tears rolled down his cheeks. In all the years I have listened to my wife sing, I never heard her the way he did at that moment.

~~~~ Marriage. Almost everyone I knew had a problem with it. Some had problems getting into it, some had problems getting out. My generation seemed to struggle with the commitment, as if it were an alligator from some murky swamp. I had gotten used to attending weddings, congratulating the couple, and feeling only mild surprise when I saw the groom a few years later sitting in a restaurant with a younger woman whom he introduced as a friend. "You know, I'm separated from so-and-so . . ." he would say.

Why do we have such problems? I asked Morrie about this. Having waited seven years before I proposed to Janine, I wondered if people my age were being more careful than those who came before us, or simply more selfish?

"Well, I feel sorry for your generation," Morrie said. "In this culture, it's so important to find a loving relationship with someone because so much of the culture does not give you that. But the poor kids today, either they're too selfish to take part in a real loving relationship, or they rush into marriage and then six months later, they get divorced. They don't know what they want in a partner. They don't know who they are themselves—so how can they know who they're marrying?"

He sighed. Morrie had counseled so many unhappy lovers in his years as a professor. "It's sad, because a loved one is so important. You realize that, especially when you're in a time like I am, when you're not doing so well. Friends are great, but friends are not going to be here on a night when you're coughing and can't sleep and someone has to sit up all night with you, comfort you, try to be helpful."

Charlotte and Morrie, who met as students, had been married forty-four years. I watched them together now, when she would remind him of his medication, or come in and stroke his neck, or talk about one of their sons. They worked as a team, often needing no more than a silent glance to understand what the other was thinking. Charlotte was a private person, different from Morrie, but I knew how much he respected her, because sometimes when we spoke, he would say, "Charlotte might be uncomfortable with me revealing that," and he would end the conversation. It was the only time Morrie held anything back.

"I've learned this much about marriage," he said now. "You get tested. You find out who you are, who the other person is, and how you accommodate or don't."

Is there some kind of rule to know if a marriage is going to work?

Morrie smiled. "Things are not that simple, Mitch."

I know.

"Still," he said, "there are a few rules I know to be true about love and marriage: If you don't respect the other person, you're gonna have a lot of trouble. If you don't know how to compromise, you're gonna have a lot of trouble. If you can't talk openly about what goes on between you, you're gonna have a lot of trouble. And if you don't have a common set of values in life, you're gonna have a lot of trouble. Your values must be alike.

"And the biggest one of those values, Mitch?"

Yes?

"Your belief in the *importance* of your marriage."

He sniffed, then closed his eyes for a moment.

"Personally," he sighed, his eyes still closed, "I think marriage is a very important thing to do, and you're missing a hell of a lot if you don't try it."

He ended the subject by quoting the poem he believed in like a prayer: "Love each other or perish."

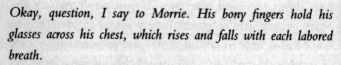

Okay, question, I say to Morrie. His bony fingers hold his glasses across his chest, which rises and falls with each labored breath.

"What's the question?" he says.

Remember the Book of Job?

"From the Bible?"

Right. Job is a good man, but God makes him suffer. To test his faith.

"I remember."

Takes away everything he has, his house, his money, his family . . .

"His health."

Makes him sick.

"To test his faith."

Right. To test his faith. So, I'm wondering . . .

"What are you wondering?"

What you think about that?

Morrie coughs violently. His hands quiver as he drops them by his side.

"I think," he says, smiling, "God overdid it."

The Eleventh Tuesday
We Talk About Our
Culture

～～ "Hit him harder."

I slapped Morrie's back.

"Harder."

I slapped him again.

"Near his shoulders . . . now down lower."

Morrie, dressed in pajama bottoms, lay in bed on his side, his head flush against the pillow, his mouth open. The physical therapist was showing me how to bang loose the poison in his lungs—which he needed done regularly now, to keep it from solidifying, to keep him breathing.

"I . . . always knew . . . you wanted . . . to hit me . . ." Morrie gasped.

Yeah, I joked as I rapped my fist against the alabaster skin of his back. This is for that B you gave me sophomore year! *Whack!*

We all laughed, a nervous laughter that comes when the devil is within earshot. It would have been cute, this little scene, were it not what we all knew it was, the final calisthenics before death. Morrie's disease was now dangerously close to his surrender spot, his lungs. He had been predicting he would die from choking, and I could not imagine a more terrible way to go. Sometimes he would close his eyes and try to draw the air up into his mouth and nostrils, and it seemed as if he were trying to lift an anchor.

Outside, it was jacket weather, early October, the leaves clumped in piles on the lawns around West Newton. Morrie's physical therapist had come earlier in the day, and I usually excused myself when nurses or specialists had business with him. But as the weeks passed and our time ran down, I was increasingly less self-conscious about the physical embarrassment. I wanted to be there. I wanted to observe everything. This was not like me, but then, neither were a lot of things that had happened these last few months in Morrie's house.

So I watched the therapist work on Morrie in the bed, pounding the back of his ribs, asking if he could feel the congestion loosening within him. And when she took a break, she asked if I wanted to try it. I said yes. Morrie, his face on the pillow, gave a little smile.

"Not too hard," he said. "I'm an old man."

I drummed on his back and sides, moving around, as she instructed. I hated the idea of Morrie's lying in bed under any circumstances (his last aphorism, "When you're in bed, you're dead," rang in my ears), and curled on his side, he was so small, so withered, it was more a boy's body than a man's. I saw the paleness of his skin, the stray white hairs, the way his arms hung limp and helpless. I thought about how much time we spend trying to shape our bodies, lifting weights, crunching sit-ups, and in the end, nature takes it away from us anyhow. Beneath my fingers, I felt the loose flesh around Morrie's bones, and I thumped him hard, as instructed. The truth is, I was pounding on his back when I wanted to be hitting the walls.

"Mitch?" Morrie gasped, his voice jumpy as a jackhammer as I pounded on him.

Uh-huh?

"When did . . . I . . . give you . . . a B?"

~~~~ Morrie believed in the inherent good of people. But he also saw what they could become.

"People are only mean when they're threatened," he said later that day, "and that's what our culture does. That's what our economy does. Even people who have jobs in our economy are threatened, because they worry about losing them. And when you get threatened, you start looking out only for yourself. You start making money a god. It is all part of this culture."

He exhaled. "Which is why I don't buy into it."

I nodded at him and squeezed his hand. We held hands regularly now. This was another change for me. Things that before would have made me embarrassed or squeamish were now routinely handled. The catheter bag,

onnected to the tube inside him and filled with greenish
waste fluid, lay by my foot near the leg of his chair. A few
months earlier, it might have disgusted me; it was inconsequential now. So was the smell of the room after Morrie
had used the commode. He did not have the luxury of
moving from place to place, of closing a bathroom door
behind him, spraying some air freshener when he left.
There was his bed, there was his chair, and that was his
life. If my life were squeezed into such a thimble, I doubt
I could make it smell any better.

"Here's what I mean by building your own little sub-
culture," Morrie said. "I don't mean you disregard every
rule of your community. I don't go around naked, for
example. I don't run through red lights. The little things,
I can obey. But the big things—how we think, what we
value—those you must choose yourself. You can't let anyone—or any society—determine those for you.

"Take my condition. The things I am supposed to be
embarrassed about now—not being able to walk, not being able to wipe my ass, waking up some mornings wanting to cry—there is nothing innately embarrassing or
shaming about them.

"It's the same for women not being thin enough, or
men not being rich enough. It's just what our culture
would have you believe. Don't believe it."

I asked Morrie why he hadn't moved somewhere else
when he was younger.

"Where?"

I don't know. South America. New Guinea. Someplace not as selfish as America.

"Every society has its own problems," Morrie said, lifting his eyebrows, the closest he could come to a shrug. "The way to do it, I think, isn't to run away. You have to work at creating your own culture.

"Look, no matter where you live, the biggest defect we human beings have is our shortsightedness. We don't see what we could be. We should be looking at our potential, stretching ourselves into everything we can become. But if you're surrounded by people who say 'I want mine now,' you end up with a few people with everything and a military to keep the poor ones from rising up and stealing it."

Morrie looked over my shoulder to the far window. Sometimes you could hear a passing truck or a whip of the wind. He gazed for a moment at his neighbors' houses, then continued.

"The problem, Mitch, is that we don't believe we are as much alike as we are. Whites and blacks, Catholics and Protestants, men and women. If we saw each other as more alike, we might be very eager to join in one big human family in this world, and to care about that family the way we care about our own.

"But believe me, when you are dying, you see it is

true. We all have the same beginning—birth—and we all have the same end—death. So how different can we be?

"Invest in the human family. Invest in people. Build a little community of those you love and who love you."

He squeezed my hand gently. I squeezed back harder. And like that carnival contest where you bang a hammer and watch the disk rise up the pole, I could almost see my body heat rise up Morrie's chest and neck into his cheeks and eyes. He smiled.

"In the beginning of life, when we are infants, we need others to survive, right? And at the end of life, when you get like me, you need others to survive, right?"

His voice dropped to a whisper. "But here's the secret: in between, we need others as well."

Later that afternoon, Connie and I went into the bedroom to watch the O. J. Simpson verdict. It was a tense scene as the principals all turned to face the jury, Simpson, in his blue suit, surrounded by his small army of lawyers, the prosecutors who wanted him behind bars just a few feet away. When the foreman read the verdict— "Not guilty"—Connie shrieked.

"Oh my God!"

We watched as Simpson hugged his lawyers. We listened as the commentators tried to explain what it all meant. We saw crowds of blacks celebrating in the streets outside the courthouse, and crowds of whites sitting stunned inside restaurants. The decision was being hailed as momentous, even though murders take place every day. Connie went out in the hall. She had seen enough.

I heard the door to Morrie's study close. I stared at the TV set. *Everyone in the world is watching this thing,* I told myself. Then, from the other room, I heard the ruffling of Morrie's being lifted from his chair and I smiled. As "The Trial of the Century" reached its dramatic conclusion, my old professor was sitting on the toilet.

It is 1979, a basketball game in the Brandeis gym. The team is doing well, and the student section begins a chant, "We're number one! We're number one!" Morrie is sitting nearby. He is puzzled by the cheer. At one point, in the midst of "We're number one!" he rises and yells, "What's wrong with being number two?"

The students look at him. They stop chanting. He sits down, smiling and triumphant.

The Audiovisual, Part Three

The "Nightline" crew came back for its third and final visit. The whole tenor of the thing was different now. Less like an interview, more like a sad farewell. Ted Koppel had called several times before coming up, and he had asked Morrie, "Do you think you can handle it?"

Morrie wasn't sure he could. "I'm tired all the time now, Ted. And I'm choking a lot. If I can't say something, will you say it for me?"

Koppel said sure. And then the normally stoic anchor added this: "If you don't want to do it, Morrie, it's okay. I'll come up and say good-bye anyhow."

Later, Morrie would grin mischievously and say, "I'm getting to him." And he was. Koppel now referred to Morrie as "a friend." My old professor had even coaxed compassion out of the television business.

For the interview, which took place on a Friday afternoon, Morrie wore the same shirt he'd had on the day before. He changed shirts only every other day at this point, and this was not the other day, so why break routine?

Unlike the previous two Koppel–Schwartz sessions,

this one was conducted entirely within Morrie's study, where Morrie had become a prisoner of his chair. Koppel, who kissed my old professor when he first saw him, now had to squeeze in alongside the bookcase in order to be seen in the camera's lens.

Before they started, Koppel asked about the disease's progression. "How bad is it, Morrie?".

Morrie weakly lifted a hand, halfway up his belly. This was as far as he could go.

Koppel had his answer.

The camera rolled, the third and final interview. Koppel asked if Morrie was more afraid now that death was near. Morrie said no; to tell the truth, he was less afraid. He said he was letting go of some of the outside world, not having the newspaper read to him as much, not paying as much attention to mail, instead listening more to music and watching the leaves change color through his window.

There were other people who suffered from ALS, Morrie knew, some of them famous, such as Stephen Hawking, the brilliant physicist and author of *A Brief History of Time*. He lived with a hole in his throat, spoke through a computer synthesizer, typed words by batting his eyes as a sensor picked up the movement.

This was admirable, but it was not the way Morrie wanted to live. He told Koppel he knew when it would be time to say good-bye.

"For me, Ted, living means I can be responsive to the other person. It means I can show my emotions and my feelings. Talk to them. Feel with them . . ."

He exhaled. "When that is gone, Morrie is gone."

They talked like friends. As he had in the previous two interviews, Koppel asked about the "old ass wipe test"—hoping, perhaps, for a humorous response. But Morrie was too tired even to grin. He shook his head. "When I sit on the commode, I can no longer sit up straight. I'm listing all the time, so they have to hold me. When I'm done they have to wipe me. That is how far it's gotten."

He told Koppel he wanted to die with serenity. He shared his latest aphorism: "Don't let go too soon, but don't hang on too long."

Koppel nodded painfully. Only six months had passed between the first "Nightline" show and this one, but Morrie Schwartz was clearly a collapsed form. He had decayed before a national TV audience, a miniseries of a death. But as his body rotted, his character shone even more brightly.

Toward the end of the interview, the camera zoomed in on Morrie—Koppel was not even in the picture, only his voice was heard from outside it—and the anchor asked if my old professor had anything he wanted to say to the millions of people he had touched. Although he did not mean it this way, I couldn't help but think of a condemned man being asked for his final words.

"Be compassionate," Morrie whispered. "And take responsibility for each other. If we only learned those lessons, this world would be so much better a place."

He took a breath, then added his mantra: "Love each other or die."

The interview was ended. But for some reason, the cameraman left the film rolling, and a final scene was caught on tape.

"You did a good job," Koppel said.

Morrie smiled weakly.

"I gave you what I had," he whispered.

"You always do."

"Ted, this disease is knocking at my spirit. But it will not get my spirit. It'll get my body. It will *not* get my spirit."

Koppel was near tears. "You done good."

"You think so?" Morrie rolled his eyes toward the ceiling. "I'm bargaining with Him up there now. I'm asking Him, 'Do I get to be one of the angels?'"

It was the first time Morrie admitted talking to God.

The Twelfth Tuesday
We Talk About Forgiveness

~~~ "Forgive yourself before you die. Then forgive others."

This was a few days after the "Nightline" interview. The sky was rainy and dark, and Morrie was beneath a blanket. I sat at the far end of his chair, holding his bare feet. They were callused and curled, and his toenails were yellow. I had a small jar of lotion, and I squeezed some into my hands and began to massage his ankles.

It was another of the things I had watched his helpers do for months, and now, in an attempt to hold on to what I could of him, I had volunteered to do it myself. The disease had left Morrie without the ability even to wiggle his toes, yet he could still feel pain, and massages helped relieve it. Also, of course, Morrie liked being held and touched. And at this point, anything I could do to make him happy, I was going to do.

"Mitch," he said, returning to the subject of forgiveness. "There is no point in keeping vengeance or stubbornness. These things"—he sighed—"these things I so regret in my life. Pride. Vanity. Why do we do the things we do?"

The importance of forgiving was my question. I had seen those movies where the patriarch of the family is on his death bed and he calls for his estranged son so that he can make peace before he goes. I wondered if Morrie had any of that inside him, a sudden need to say "I'm sorry" before he died?

Morrie nodded. "Do you see that sculpture?" He tilted his head toward a bust that sat high on a shelf against the far wall of his office. I had never really noticed it before. Cast in bronze, it was the face of a man in his early forties, wearing a necktie, a tuft of hair falling across his forehead.

"That's me," Morrie said. "A friend of mine sculpted that maybe thirty years ago. His name was Norman. We used to spend so much time together. We went swimming. We took rides to New York. He had me over to his house in Cambridge, and he sculpted that bust of me down in his basement. It took several weeks to do it, but he really wanted to get it right."

I studied the face. How strange to see a three-dimensional Morrie, so healthy, so young, watching over us as we spoke. Even in bronze, he had a whimsical look, and I thought this friend had sculpted a little spirit as well.

"Well, here's the sad part of the story," Morrie said. "Norman and his wife moved away to Chicago. A little while later, my wife, Charlotte, had to have a pretty serious operation. Norman and his wife never got in touch with us. I know they knew about it. Charlotte and I were very hurt because they never called to see how she was. So we dropped the relationship.

"Over the years, I met Norman a few times and he always tried to reconcile, but I didn't accept it. I wasn't satisfied with his explanation. I was prideful. I shrugged him off."

His voice choked.

"Mitch . . . a few years ago . . . he died of cancer. I feel so sad. I never got to see him. I never got to forgive. It pains me now so much . . ."

He was crying again, a soft and quiet cry, and because his head was back, the tears rolled off the side of his face before they reached his lips.

Sorry, I said.

"Don't be," he whispered. "Tears are okay."

I continued rubbing lotion into his lifeless toes. He wept for a few minutes, alone with his memories.

"It's not just other people we need to forgive, Mitch," he finally whispered. "We also need to forgive ourselves."

Ourselves?

"Yes. For all the things we didn't do. All the things we should have done. You can't get stuck on the regrets of what should have happened. That doesn't help you when you get to where I am.

"I always wished I had done more with my work; I

wished I had written more books. I used to beat myself up over it. Now I see that never did any good. Make peace. You need to make peace with yourself and everyone around you."

I leaned over and dabbed at the tears with a tissue. Morrie flicked his eyes open and closed. His breathing was audible, like a light snore.

"Forgive yourself. Forgive others. Don't wait, Mitch. Not everyone gets the time I'm getting. Not everyone is as lucky."

I tossed the tissue into the wastebasket and returned to his feet. Lucky? I pressed my thumb into his hardened flesh and he didn't even feel it.

"The tension of opposites, Mitch. Remember that? Things pulling in different directions?"

I remember.

"I mourn my dwindling time, but I cherish the chance it gives me to make things right."

We sat there for a while, quietly, as the rain splattered against the windows. The hibiscus plant behind his head was still holding on, small but firm.

"Mitch," Morrie whispered.

Uh-huh?

I rolled his toes between my fingers, lost in the task.

"Look at me."

I glanced up and saw the most intense look in his eyes.

"I don't know why you came back to me. But I want to say this . . ."

He paused, and his voice choked.

"If I could have had another son, I would have liked it to be you."

I dropped my eyes, kneading the dying flesh of his feet between my fingers. For a moment, I felt afraid, as if accepting his words would somehow betray my own father. But when I looked up, I saw Morrie smiling through tears and I knew there was no betrayal in a moment like this.

All I was afraid of was saying good-bye.

"I've picked a place to be buried."

Where is that?

"Not far from here. On a hill, beneath a tree, overlooking a pond. Very serene. A good place to think."

Are you planning on thinking there?

"I'm planning on being dead there."

He chuckles. I chuckle.

"Will you visit?"

Visit?

"Just come and talk. Make it a Tuesday. You always come on Tuesdays."

We're Tuesday people.

"Right. Tuesday people. Come to talk, then?"

He has grown so weak so fast.

"Look at me," he says.

I'm looking.

"You'll come to my grave? To tell me your problems?"

My problems?

"Yes."

And you'll give me answers?

"I'll give you what I can. Don't I always?"

I picture his grave, on the hill, overlooking the pond, some little nine-foot piece of earth where they will place him, cover him with dirt, put a stone on top. Maybe in a few weeks? Maybe in a few days? I see myself sitting there alone, arms across my knees, staring into space.

It won't be the same, I say, not being able to hear you talk.

"Ah, talk . . ."

He closes his eyes and smiles.

"Tell you what. After I'm dead, you talk. And I'll listen."

The Thirteenth Tuesday
We Talk About the Perfect Day

～ Morrie wanted to be cremated. He had discussed it with Charlotte, and they decided it was the best way. The rabbi from Brandeis, Al Axelrad—a longtime friend whom they chose to conduct the funeral service—had come to visit Morrie, and Morrie told him of his cremation plans.

"And Al?"

"Yes?"

"Make sure they don't overcook me."

The rabbi was stunned. But Morrie was able to joke about his body now. The closer he got to the end, the more he saw it as a mere shell, a container of the soul. It was withering to useless skin and bones anyhow, which made it easier to let go.

"We are so afraid of the sight of death," Morrie told me when I sat down. I adjusted the microphone on his collar, but it kept flopping over. Morrie coughed. He was coughing all the time now.

"I read a book the other day. It said as soon as someone dies in a hospital, they pull the sheets up over their head, and they wheel the body to some chute and push it down. They can't wait to get it out of their sight. People act as if death is contagious."

I fumbled with the microphone. Morrie glanced at my hands.

"It's not contagious, you know. Death is as natural as life. It's part of the deal we made."

He coughed again, and I moved back and waited, always braced for something serious. Morrie had been having bad nights lately. Frightening nights. He could sleep only a few hours at a time before violent hacking spells woke him. The nurses would come into the bedroom, pound him on the back, try to bring up the poison. Even if they got him breathing normally again—"normally" meaning with the help of the oxygen machine—the fight left him fatigued the whole next day.

The oxygen tube was up his nose now. I hated the sight of it. To me, it symbolized helplessness. I wanted to pull it out.

"Last night . . ." Morrie said softly.

Yes? Last night?

". . . I had a terrible spell. It went on for hours. And I really wasn't sure I was going to make it. No breath. No end to the choking. At one point, I started to get dizzy . . . and then I felt a certain peace, I felt that I was ready to go."

His eyes widened. "Mitch, it was a most incredible feeling. The sensation of accepting what was happening, being at peace. I was thinking about a dream I had last week, where I was crossing a bridge into something unknown. Being ready to move on to whatever is next."

But you didn't.

Morrie waited a moment. He shook his head slightly. "No, I didn't. But I felt that I *could*. Do you understand?

"That's what we're all looking for. A certain peace with the idea of dying. If we know, in the end, that we can ultimately have that peace with dying, then we can finally do the really hard thing."

Which is?

"Make peace with living."

He asked to see the hibiscus plant on the ledge behind him. I cupped it in my hand and held it up near his eyes. He smiled.

"It's natural to die," he said again. "The fact that we make such a big hullabaloo over it is all because we don't see ourselves as part of nature. We think because we're human we're something above nature."

He smiled at the plant.

"We're not. Everything that gets born, dies." He looked at me.

"Do you accept that?"

Yes.

"All right," he whispered, "now here's the payoff. Here is how we *are* different from these wonderful plants and animals.

"As long as we can love each other, and remember the feeling of love we had, we can die without ever really going away. All the love you created is still there. All the memories are still there. You live on—in the hearts of everyone you have touched and nurtured while you were here."

His voice was raspy, which usually meant he needed to stop for a while. I placed the plant back on the ledge and went to shut off the tape recorder. This is the last sentence Morrie got out before I did:

"Death ends a life, not a relationship."

There had been a development in the treatment of ALS: an experimental drug that was just gaining passage. It was not a cure, but a delay, a slowing of the decay for perhaps a few months. Morrie had heard about it, but he was too far gone. Besides, the medicine wouldn't be available for several months.

"Not for me," Morrie said, dismissing it.

In all the time he was sick, Morrie never held out hope he would be cured. He was realistic to a fault. One time, I asked if someone were to wave a magic wand and make him all better, would he become, in time, the man he had been before?

He shook his head. "No way I could go back. I am a

different self now. I'm different in my attitudes. I'm different appreciating my body, which I didn't do fully before. I'm different in terms of trying to grapple with the big questions, the ultimate questions, the ones that won't go away.

"That's the thing, you see. Once you get your fingers on the important questions, you can't turn away from them."

And which are the important questions?

"As I see it, they have to do with love, responsibility, spirituality, awareness. And if I were healthy today, those would still be my issues. They should have been all along."

I tried to imagine Morrie healthy. I tried to imagine him pulling the covers from his body, stepping from that chair, the two of us going for a walk around the neighborhood, the way we used to walk around campus. I suddenly realized it had been sixteen years since I'd seen him standing up. Sixteen years?

What if you had one day perfectly healthy, I asked? What would you do?

"Twenty-four hours?"

Twenty-four hours.

"Let's see . . . I'd get up in the morning, do my exercises, have a lovely breakfast of sweet rolls and tea, go for a swim, then have my friends come over for a nice lunch. I'd have them come one or two at a time so we could talk about their families, their issues, talk about how much we mean to each other.

"Then I'd like to go for a walk, in a garden with some trees, watch their colors, watch the birds, take in the nature that I haven't seen in so long now.

"In the evening, we'd all go together to a restaurant with some great pasta, maybe some duck—I love duck—and then we'd dance the rest of the night. I'd dance with all the wonderful dance partners out there, until I was exhausted. And then I'd go home and have a deep, wonderful sleep."

That's it?

"That's it."

It was so simple. So average. I was actually a little disappointed. I figured he'd fly to Italy or have lunch with the President or romp on the seashore or try every exotic thing he could think of. After all these months, lying there, unable to move a leg or a foot—how could he find perfection in such an average day?

Then I realized this was the whole point.

Before I left that day, Morrie asked if *he* could bring up a topic.

"Your brother," he said.

I felt a shiver. I do not know how Morrie knew this was on my mind. I had been trying to call my brother in Spain for weeks, and had learned—from a friend of his—that he was flying back and forth to a hospital in Amsterdam.

"Mitch, I know it hurts when you can't be with someone you love. But you need to be at peace with his desires. Maybe he doesn't want you interrupting your life. Maybe he can't deal with that burden. I tell everyone I know to carry on with the life they know—don't ruin it because I am dying."

But he's my brother, I said.

"I know," Morrie said. "That's why it hurts."

I saw Peter in my mind when he was eight years old, his curly blond hair puffed into a sweaty ball atop his head. I saw us wrestling in the yard next to our house, the grass stains soaking through the knees of our jeans. I saw him singing songs in front of the mirror, holding a brush as a microphone, and I saw us squeezing into the attic where we hid together as children, testing our parents' will to find us for dinner.

And then I saw him as the adult who had drifted away, thin and frail, his face bony from the chemotherapy treatments.

Morrie, I said. Why doesn't he want to see me?

My old professor sighed. "There is no formula to

relationships. They have to be negotiated in loving ways, with room for both parties, what they want and what they need, what they can do and what their life is like.

"In business, people negotiate to win. They negotiate to get what they want. Maybe you're too used to that. Love is different. Love is when you are as concerned about someone else's situation as you are about your own.

"You've had these special times with your brother, and you no longer have what you had with him. You want them back. You never want them to stop. But that's part of being human. Stop, renew, stop, renew."

I looked at him. I saw all the death in the world. I felt helpless.

"You'll find a way back to your brother," Morrie said.

How do you know?

Morrie smiled. "You found me, didn't you?"

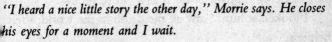

"I heard a nice little story the other day," Morrie says. He closes his eyes for a moment and I wait.

"Okay. The story is about a little wave, bobbing along in the ocean, having a grand old time. He's enjoying the wind and the fresh air—until he notices the other waves in front of him, crashing against the shore.

" 'My God, this is terrible,' the wave says. 'Look what's going to happen to me!'

"Then along comes another wave. It sees the first wave, looking grim, and it says to him, 'Why do you look so sad?'

"The first wave says, 'You don't understand! We're all going to crash! All of us waves are going to be nothing! Isn't it terrible?'

"The second wave says, 'No, you don't understand. You're not a wave, you're part of the ocean.'"

I smile. Morrie closes his eyes again.

"Part of the ocean," he says, "part of the ocean." I watch him breathe, in and out, in and out.

The Fourteenth Tuesday
We Say Good-bye

~~~~ It was cold and damp as I walked up the steps to Morrie's house. I took in little details, things I hadn't noticed for all the times I'd visited. The cut of the hill. The stone facade of the house. The pachysandra plants, the low shrubs. I walked slowly, taking my time, stepping on dead wet leaves that flattened beneath my feet.

Charlotte had called the day before to tell me Morrie "was not doing well." This was her way of saying the final days had arrived. Morrie had canceled all of his appointments and had been sleeping much of the time, which was unlike him. He never cared for sleeping, not when there were people he could talk with.

"He wants you to come visit," Charlotte said, "but, Mitch . . ."

Yes?

"He's very weak."

The porch steps. The glass in the front door. I absorbed these things in a slow, observant manner, as if seeing them for the first time. I felt the tape recorder in the bag on my shoulder, and I unzipped it to make sure I had tapes. I don't know why. I always had tapes.

Connie answered the bell. Normally buoyant, she had a drawn look on her face. Her hello was softly spoken.

"How's he doing?" I said.

"Not so good." She bit her lower lip. "I don't like to think about it. He's such a sweet man, you know?"

I knew.

"This is such a shame."

Charlotte came down the hall and hugged me. She said that Morrie was still sleeping, even though it was 10 A.M. We went into the kitchen. I helped her straighten up, noticing all the bottles of pills, lined up on the table, a small army of brown plastic soldiers with white caps. My old professor was taking morphine now to ease his breathing.

I put the food I had brought with me into the refrigerator—soup, vegetable cakes, tuna salad. I apologized to Charlotte for bringing it. Morrie hadn't chewed food like this in months, we both knew that, but it had become a small tradition. Sometimes, when you're losing someone, you hang on to whatever tradition you can.

I waited in the living room, where Morrie and Ted Koppel had done their first interview. I read the newspaper that was lying on the table. Two Minnesota children had shot each other playing with their fathers' guns. A baby had been found buried in a garbage can in an alley in Los Angeles.

I put down the paper and stared into the empty fireplace. I tapped my shoe lightly on the hardwood floor. Eventually, I heard a door open and close, then Charlotte's footsteps coming toward me.

"All right," she said softly. "He's ready for you."

I rose and I turned toward our familiar spot, then saw a strange woman sitting at the end of the hall in a folding chair, her eyes on a book, her legs crossed. This was a hospice nurse, part of the twenty-four-hour watch.

Morrie's study was empty. I was confused. Then I turned back hesitantly to the bedroom, and there he was, lying in bed, under the sheet. I had seen him like this only one other time—when he was getting massaged—and the echo of his aphorism "When you're in bed, you're dead" began anew inside my head.

I entered, pushing a smile onto my face. He wore a yellow pajama-like top, and a blanket covered him from the chest down. The lump of his form was so withered that I almost thought there was something missing. He was as small as a child.

Morrie's mouth was open, and his skin was pale and tight against his cheekbones. When his eyes rolled toward me, he tried to speak, but I heard only a soft grunt.

There he is, I said, mustering all the excitement I could find in my empty till.

He exhaled, shut his eyes, then smiled, the very effort seeming to tire him.

"My . . . dear friend . . ." he finally said.

I am your friend, I said.

"I'm not . . . so good today . . ."

Tomorrow will be better.

He pushed out another breath and forced a nod. He was struggling with something beneath the sheets, and I realized he was trying to move his hands toward the opening.

"Hold . . ." he said.

I pulled the covers down and grasped his fingers. They disappeared inside my own. I leaned in close, a few inches from his face. It was the first time I had seen him unshaven, the small white whiskers looking so out of place, as if someone had shaken salt neatly across his cheeks and chin. How could there be new life in his beard when it was draining everywhere else?

Morrie, I said softly.

"Coach," he corrected.

Coach, I said. I felt a shiver. He spoke in short bursts, inhaling air, exhaling words. His voice was thin and raspy. He smelled of ointment.

"You . . . are a good soul."

A good soul.

"Touched me . . ." he whispered. He moved my hands to his heart. "Here."

It felt as if I had a pit in my throat.

Coach?

"Ahh?"

I don't know how to say good-bye.

He patted my hand weakly, keeping it on his chest.

"This . . . is how we say . . . good-bye . . ."

He breathed softly, in and out, I could feel his rib-cage rise and fall. Then he looked right at me.

"Love . . . you," he rasped.

I love you, too, Coach.

"Know   you   do . . . know . . . something else . . ."

What else do you know?

"You . . . always have . . ."

His eyes got small, and then he cried, his face con-torting like a baby who hasn't figured how his tear ducts work. I held him close for several minutes. I rubbed his loose skin. I stroked his hair. I put a palm against his face and felt the bones close to the flesh and the tiny wet tears, as if squeezed from a dropper.

When his breathing approached normal again, I cleared my throat and said I knew he was tired, so I would be back next Tuesday, and I expected him to be a little more alert, thank you. He snorted lightly, as close as he could come to a laugh. It was a sad sound just the same.

I picked up the unopened bag with the tape recorder. Why had I even brought this? I knew we would never use it. I leaned in and kissed him closely, my face against his, whiskers on whiskers, skin on skin, holding it there, longer than normal, in case it gave him even a split second of pleasure.

Okay, then? I said, pulling away.

I blinked back the tears, and he smacked his lips together and raised his eyebrows at the sight of my face. I like to think it was a fleeting moment of satisfaction for my dear old professor: he had finally made me cry.

"Okay, then," he whispered.

Graduation

～⌒ Morrie died on a Saturday morning.

His immediate family was with him in the house. Rob made it in from Tokyo—he got to kiss his father good-bye—and Jon was there, and of course Charlotte was there and Charlotte's cousin Marsha, who had written the poem that so moved Morrie at his "unofficial" memorial service, the poem that likened him to a "tender sequoia." They slept in shifts around his bed. Morrie had fallen into a coma two days after our final visit, and the doctor said he could go at any moment. Instead, he hung on, through a tough afternoon, through a dark night.

Finally, on the fourth of November, when those he loved had left the room just for a moment—to grab coffee in the kitchen, the first time none of them were with him since the coma began—Morrie stopped breathing.

And he was gone.

I believe he died this way on purpose. I believe he wanted no chilling moments, no one to witness his last breath and be haunted by it, the way he had been haunted by his mother's death-notice telegram or by his father's corpse in the city morgue.

I believe he knew that he was in his own bed, that his books and his notes and his small hibiscus plant were nearby. He wanted to go serenely, and that is how he went.

The funeral was held on a damp, windy morning. The grass was wet and the sky was the color of milk. We stood by the hole in the earth, close enough to hear the pond water lapping against the edge and to see ducks shaking off their feathers.

Although hundreds of people had wanted to attend, Charlotte kept this gathering small, just a few close friends and relatives. Rabbi Axelrod read a few poems. Morrie's brother, David—who still walked with a limp from his childhood polio—lifted the shovel and tossed dirt in the grave, as per tradition.

At one point, when Morrie's ashes were placed into the ground, I glanced around the cemetery. Morrie was right. It was indeed a lovely spot, trees and grass and a sloping hill.

"You talk, I'll listen," he had said.

I tried doing that in my head and, to my happiness, found that the imagined conversation felt almost natural. I looked down at my hands, saw my watch and realized why.

It was Tuesday.

"My father moved through theys of we,
singing each new leaf out of each tree
(and every child was sure that spring
danced when she heard my father sing) . . ."

—A POEM BY E. E. CUMMINGS, READ BY MORRIE'S SON, ROB, AT THE
MEMORIAL SERVICE

Conclusion

I look back sometimes at the person I was before I rediscovered my old professor. I want to talk to that person. I want to tell him what to look out for, what mistakes to avoid. I want to tell him to be more open, to ignore the lure of advertised values, to pay attention when your loved ones are speaking, as if it were the last time you might hear them.

Mostly I want to tell that person to get on an airplane and visit a gentle old man in West Newton, Massachusetts, sooner rather than later, before that old man gets sick and loses his ability to dance.

I know I cannot do this. None of us can undo what we've done, or relive a life already recorded. But if Professor Morris Schwartz taught me anything at all, it was this: there is no such thing as "too late" in life. He was changing until the day he said good-bye.

Not long after Morrie's death, I reached my brother in Spain. We had a long talk. I told him I respected his distance, and that all I wanted was to be in touch—in the present, not just the past—to hold him in my life as much as he could let me.

"You're my only brother," I said. "I don't want to lose you. I love you."

I had never said such a thing to him before.

A few days later, I received a message on my fax machine. It was typed in the sprawling, poorly punctuated, all-cap-letters fashion that always characterized my brother's words.

"HI I'VE JOINED THE NINETIES!" it began. He wrote a few little stories, what he'd been doing that week, a couple of jokes. At the end, he signed off this way:

I HAVE HEARTBURN AND DIAHREA AT THE MOMENT—LIFE'S A BITCH. CHAT LATER?
[signed]   SORE TUSH.

I laughed until there were tears in my eyes.

This book was largely Morrie's idea. He called it our "final thesis." Like the best of work projects, it brought us closer together, and Morrie was delighted when several publishers expressed interest, even though he died before meeting any of them. The advance money helped pay Morrie's enormous medical bills, and for that we were both grateful.

The title, by the way, we came up with one day in Morrie's office. He liked naming things. He had several ideas. But when I said, "How about *Tuesdays with Morrie*?" he smiled in an almost blushing way, and I knew that was it.

After Morrie died, I went through boxes of old college material. And I discovered a final paper I had written for one of his classes. It was twenty years old now. On the front page were my penciled comments scribbled to Morrie, and beneath them were his comments scribbled back.

Mine began, "Dear Coach . . ."

His began, "Dear Player . . ."

For some reason, each time I read that, I miss him more.

Have you ever really had a teacher? One who saw you as a raw but precious thing, a jewel that, with wisdom, could be polished to a proud shine? If you are lucky enough to find your way to such teachers, you will always find your way back. Sometimes it is only in your head. Sometimes it is right alongside their beds.

The last class of my old professor's life took place once a week, in his home, by a window in his study where he could watch a small hibiscus plant shed its pink flowers. The class met on Tuesdays. No books were required. The subject was the meaning of life. It was taught from experience.

The teaching goes on.

Warner Books now offers an exciting range of quality titles by both established and new authors. All of the books in this series are available from:

Warner Books
P.O. Box 121, Kettering,
Northants NN14 4ZQ

Fax No: 01832 733076
Telephone No: 01832 737525
Email: aspenhouse@FSBDial.co.uk

Payments can be made as follows: cheque, postal order (payable to Warner Books) or by credit cards, Visa/Access. Do not send cash or currency. All U.K. orders free of charge. E.E.C. and Overseas: 25% of order value.

NAME (Block Letters) ....

....

ADDRESS ....

....

....

☐ I enclose my remittance for ....

☐ I wish to pay by Access/Visa Card ....

Number ☐☐☐☐☐☐☐☐☐☐☐☐☐☐☐☐

Card Expiry Date ☐☐☐☐

"Accessible, jargon-free and dealing with a struggle that women are very prone to, this will be a really helpful book for encouraging women to find their way out of a comparison-driven life."

KATHY KELLER, co-author of The Meaning of Marriage

"This book is simple but profound—and profoundly helpful. The common problem of comparison is exposed for what it is. In its place comes biblical truth, giving life and health and wholeness."

GRAHAM BEYNON, author of Mirror Mirror and Emotions

"We all know we compare ourselves with others. Sophie exposes the reasons why through clear biblical analysis, and I could not wait to read about the treatment. It is a real page-turner—a book to read and then read again."

ANN BENTON, author and conference speaker

"This moving and compassionate book analyses some of our deepest feelings from the point of view of God's word. It is confronting in places, but it points us to true contentment. I warmly commend it."

CHRISTINE JENSEN, President of the Australian Mothers' Union

"We all need help to take our eyes off the gifts we do or don't have, so we can turn our gaze to the Gift-giver Himself. This book is a helpful guide for that process—it's compassionate, honest, and truthful."

CAROLYN MCCULLEY, author of "Radical Womanhood" and conference speaker

"Sophie's examples are often funny, sometimes sad and always to the point. She takes us to God's word, showing how to turn our attention to Christ. A must-read for women of all ages."

BEULAH RETIEF, Dean of Women at George Whitefield College in Cape Town, South Africa

"I started this book assuming that it was written for other women. Within a few pages, I had started to recognise myself from the symptoms Sophie described. Full of clear insights, biblical wisdom and gospel hope, this is a book that every Christian woman should read."

ELSPETH PITT, women's worker at St Helen's Bishopsgate, London

"In an age where we so often become the source of our own pain, heartache and discouragement, this book is a must read in helping us to unleash ourselves from ourselves."

SARIE KING, conference speaker and blogger

Sophie de Witt

COMPARED To Her

How to experience true contentment

thegoodbook
COMPANY

Compared To Her *How to experience true contentment*
© Sophie de Witt/The Good Book Company, 2012.
  Reprinted 2013, 2014, 2015, 2018, 2020.

Published by:
The Good Book Company

thegoodbook.com | www.thegoodbook.co.uk
thegoodbook.com.au | thegoodbook.co.nz | thegoodbook.co.in

Unless indicated, all Scripture references are taken from the Holy Bible, New
International Version. Copyright © 2011 Biblica, Inc. Used by permission.

ISBN: 9781908762429 | Printed in India

Design by André Parker | Cover design by ninefootone creative

CONTENTS

To my precious daughter, Molly.
May you find true contentment in our Lord Jesus Christ.

INTRODUCTION

I am a recovering CCS sufferer. I'm not completely rid of it, though since recognising the problem, I've started to get better. And I know that one day, I'll be free of it. My CCS—or, to give it its full name, Compulsive Comparison Syndrome—will be a thing of the past.

But since realising I was suffering from this syndrome, I've started talking to other women about it; and I've discovered that CCS is far more widespread than I had ever imagined. As I described my symptoms to others, they realized they were struggling with a perspective dominated by CCS, too.

In fact, although I don't know you at all, I'm fairly sure that you have CCS. That's not meant to sound rude! It's just that I've rarely met a woman who doesn't struggle with it.

And as we'll see, CCS promises us contentment, but it robs us of it. So I hope that, whoever you are, you'll find that as this book explains how to be free of this syndrome, you'll also discover how you can experience real, lasting contentment in your life: with who you are, what you're doing, and where you're heading.

We'll start by looking at our lives and spotting the symptoms and triggers of CCS. Then we'll move on to see what the Bible has to say about what causes it, and how it can be treated. And we'll end by thinking about how to live healthy and contented lives without CCS.

You've probably not heard of CCS before. But the chances are you'll recognise its effects in your life. Read on…

WHAT IS CCS?

"I put on an outfit I know I look good in, and I feel great—until I get to the party. Then I see someone who looks slimmer, or cooler, or classier; suddenly the woman looking back at me in the mirror looks fat, frumpy and dull. I just want to go home."

"I'm a hard worker. I like knowing that I'm more conscientious than my co-workers. But I also find myself feeling resentful that they get away with doing so much less than me."

"I'm 28, and single. I'm usually OK with it, until a friend gets engaged or I go to a wedding. Then I find myself thinking: 'Why them? Why not me? What is wrong with me?'"

"My boyfriend loves me, I know that. But his ex-girlfriend, who dumped him, is much more attractive than me. I can't help thinking: 'If only I looked and dressed like her, then I'd really know that he really wants to be with me, and would pick me over her if he had the choice.'"

"I look at photos of myself from decades ago and feel so despondent. I used to be so much slimmer, with smooth

9

*skin and no grey hair. Mind you, at the time I thought I
was blobby and had frizzy hair…"*

*"It's always such an encouragement when I pick the kids
up from a party and someone says how they were the best-
behaved there. I'm proud of the way we brought them up;
and I'm pleased that other people notice."*

*"We don't spend much money—we're good at budgeting
and finding deals. We know people who spend their
money on all kinds of things they don't really need. I'm
glad we don't splash the cash like they do."*

*"Other women seem so caught up in keeping up with what
others are doing. I don't let myself get pulled into all that.
I'm proud that I'm just me."*

One place it happens to me is in a shopping centre. When
another woman around the same age as me passes by, I
give them a quick up-and-down scan. It's just a two-second
appraisal. And as I look at them, I see that they're doing the
same thing with me—a quick sideways glance.

What are we doing? We're comparing ourselves with each
other. How does my figure match up with hers? Does she look
more or less stylish/cool/effortless than me? Do I look as good
as her without having spent the money she clearly has? On all
these measuring scales, do I win, compared to her? Or lose?

Maybe for you it's not other women in shops. But you'll still
do that glance of comparison. It might happen in someone
else's house. Or in the bar. Or on the beach. Or at the office
or lecture hall. Or even at church, if you go. We spend our
lives making these sorts of comparisons: measuring ourselves
against others.

That's the sort of comparing that this book is about. And it's a compulsive kind of comparison; we keep on doing it. It's what I've labelled Compulsive Comparison Syndrome.

Why do we do it?

Pause for a moment before reading on, and just ask yourself:
When I compare myself with someone else, why do I do it?
What am I hoping to get out of it?

Maybe you had one of these answers, or something like it:

- *I don't know; I just do it (it's an unthinking compulsion).*
- *Because I want to know how I'm doing in life. Am I doing as well as I could be, or is there more I need to get or do?*
- *I want to make sure that I'm "normal".*
- *I need to make sure that I'm not missing out on something that others are enjoying.*
- *It makes me feel better when I realise I'm doing something better than someone else.*
- *Because my parents told me throughout my childhood to be a little bit more like my sister/other people's children.*

Underneath each of those answers to the question "Why compare?" is one of three motivations:

- *I want to know I'm worthwhile (I want to know I'm significant).*
- *I want to know that my life is as good as it could be (I want to be satisfied).*
- *I want to know that I've got what I need in life (I want to feel secure).*

Of course, sometimes it's a mixture of all three. Essentially, what I'm after is to make sure I've got as much, or more, of something than others, so that I can feel significant about who I am, satisfied about what I'm doing and secure about where I'm heading. CCS is a compulsive measuring of myself against the standards of others, desiring a higher position.

Who do we do it with?

Who was the last person you looked at and thought:

"I wish I had her…"?

How about:

"I'm so glad I'm not like her when it comes to…"

I'll compare myself with anyone. Strangers in a shopping centre, as I've said. Airbrushed models in a magazine. The owners of the houses on home improvement shows.

But most often, since they're most similar to me and I see their lives in detail most often, it's my friends, my family, the people I see most days. After all, when I compare my face to Angelina Jolie's, I've got several ready-made excuses: her skincare budget is probably more than our annual income; and, of course, she's probably been airbrushed. In my mind, she's in a different world to me. When I compare my children's behaviour to the kids of my friend who lives down the street, however, I don't have the same excuses. She's part of my world, and so that comparison has more of an effect on me.

But we can also compare ourselves with people who don't exist. Ever caught yourself comparing who you are now with who you were twenty years ago, or comparing yourself with who you dreamed you'd become, or with other people's expectations of you?

It seems to me that most of us are comparing ourselves with others all the time, in all kinds of ways. That's the problem with a compulsion; it happens unconsciously, without us even really noticing it's happening.

But we do notice the feelings the comparisons produce— the symptoms of CCS.

SYMPTOMS

The way we spot the existence of CCS in us is via the signs—the feelings—it produces.

Think of a measure you use to compare. It could be looks... or career... or partner... or DIY... or pet care (it could be anything!). When you compare yourself with someone and they come off better than you, how do you *feel?* And when you compare yourself with someone and come off better than them, what *feelings* does that produce?

When we compare ourselves with others, we'll either "lose" or "win". If we lose, we'll find ourselves doing a "looking-up comparison". We might think: "Her children are so much better behaved than mine" or: "She's so much more confident than me" or: "I wish I had her house".

If we win, then we'll do a "looking-down comparison". "My kids have better manners than hers"; "I'm glad I'm not as graceless as she is"; "I'd never let my house get into that state". And looking-up comparisons and looking-down comparisons each produce a different set of symptoms...

Looking up

How do you feel when you compare and come off worse? Let me tell you the symptoms it produces in me; perhaps you'll recognise some of them in yourself:

Inadequacy, despair, self-pity

It may be a fleeting sense—or a profound, overwhelming feeling. You're not the person you could be, should be, or want to be. You're just not good enough. And you never will be. There's no point in trying. What makes you feel like that?

Envy

It's not fair. They've got what you want—so you want what they've got. And you dislike them a little for having it. Deep down, you'd rather that neither of you had it than that they had it and you didn't. How come they get to have what you need to be significant, or satisfied, or secure?

Anxiety, insecurity

You're not doing as well as others. And so you don't have what you need to cope with life. How can you possibly cope with what tomorrow throws at you? Your pulse races and you feel the tears well up whenever you think about the future. If only you were as confident, or wealthy, or energetic, or loved-up as that friend or co-worker, there'd be no need to worry. But you're not.

Guilt

You've let others down. You're not the daughter, or wife, or mother you should be. Your family, friends or co-workers need you to be as good as the person you're comparing yourself with—but you're not. You're failing those you love. So perhaps they won't keep loving you now…

Bitterness, grumbling

We can get bitter with other people, and grumble about all sorts of things. But in the Bible, bitterness and grumbling tend to be directed at God, and that's how I'm using these two words in this book. So bitterness is thinking: "Why did God give me this life, when He has given so much more to others?" "Why did He hold back what I need to be happy, or useful, or secure?" And bitterness tends to lead to grumbling to Him: "God, if You knew what You were doing, You'd have made me more like that other woman. If You really loved me, You wouldn't have given me this unfair deal in life."

Or it leads to us ignoring God altogether—because if there were a God, He wouldn't have made you like this, and given you this life. If there is a good God, He'd have made you more like that other person.

These feelings are all symptoms of looking-up comparison. None of them are ways we would like to feel. If you're seeing yourself in many of those, it can be quite upsetting. But you're not alone, although it can seem that way because we all tend to hide our looking-up symptoms from each other. And be encouraged that there is a chapter later in this book headed "Treatment"!

Looking down

But isn't the treatment for looking-up symptoms simply to get ourselves a life which means that, when we compare ourselves to others, we come off better?

Not really… Here are the symptoms of looking-down comparisons:

Pride, arrogance

You're just so much better than that other woman. You'd just never let your hair/house/husband look like that. Deep down, you're relieved you don't suffer from their awkwardness, their dress sense, their lack of self-discipline. Well done you, for getting yourself the life you have. On your own merits, you've done so much better.

When we see this kind of self-sufficient self-congratulation in others, we usually call it "arrogance". When I see it in myself, I like to call it "self-confidence"! The Bible usually labels it "pride".

Superiority

Pride in yourself leads to a sense of superiority over others. After all, you've got what she hasn't, so you are, in a sense, better than her, aren't you? You meet standards that she simply doesn't. You're glad you're not like her.

Again, when I see this in myself, I call it "discernment". In others, I label it as what it is: judgmentalism.

Inverted superiority

You're glad you're not as arrogant as her, and don't look down on others in the way that she does. You're relieved your family isn't as flashy or stuck-up or prejudiced as theirs. You feel superior that you don't feel so superior as them!

Entitlement

Since you're better than others, you deserve better than others. When it comes to God, He ought to give you good things in this life. After all, you deserve it—you're a decent person, or you do good things each day, or you stick to religious rules. And you know you're doing well at this, because others don't do it as well as you.

Insecurity and anxiety

You're doing better than her… but how about the next person you compare yourself with? What if they're doing better than you?

Or what if you lose the possession or circumstance or quality that allows you to compare well to others? It only takes illness, or injury, or bereavement, or a financial crash and you'll lose everything that makes you you. And any of those things could happen tomorrow. Of course you're anxious, deep down!

Looking up and down

The insecure feeling that goes with looking-down comparisons is an indication of the reality that, for almost all of us, we experience both looking-up and looking-down symptoms all the time. We're a constant mixture of despair, envy, and bitterness; and pride, superiority, and entitlement. Here's how it works:

> "*My house can feel either like a dingy pokey cottage or a luxurious mansion, depending on who I've just visited. If I've just been in a large, immaculate home, I come home and think: 'What a dump'. At other times, I come home and think how well we've done to have*

our house. It's the same house but it can feel completely different on different days!"

"I help lead a youth group. I feel so envious of the other, cooler leaders—the teenagers like them so much more than me. So to try to get over my envy, I look down on the teenagers for being so shallow and appearance-focused."

Each day, we look up and we look down, and feel anxious and self-sufficient, guilty and proud, despairing and smug. What we don't feel, at least not for any length of time, is the sense of significance, satisfaction or security that we're searching for as we compare ourselves with others.

CCS promises much, which is why I glance at the woman walking towards me. But it delivers nothing, or worse than nothing. As the Bible puts it:

> *When [people] measure themselves by one another and compare themselves with one another, they are without understanding [or "wisdom"].*
>
> *(2 Corinthians chapter 10 verse 12, ESV translation)*

CCS leaves me walking away from that woman I glanced at in the shopping centre feeling arrogance, or superiority, or envy and despair. And I didn't want to experience any of those emotions!

Sound familiar?

TRIGGERS

I have a friend who is allergic to peanuts. Eating one won't kill her; but it will make her go red, sweat profusely, and swell up in her face and throat.

Of course, most of the time she is absolutely fine. If she steers clear of nuts, these rather embarrassing symptoms aren't triggered. But put a nut in her mouth, and it sets it all off.

It's the same with CCS. Some days, we're fine, but on others something triggers a whole group of those symptoms. So what are the triggers of CCS? They come in five general categories:

- *Image*
- *Circumstances*
- *Achievements*
- *Goodness*
- *Christian-ness*

Image

"Sometimes I look in the mirror and really hate the way I look; but actually my worst trigger for self-loathing is not the mirror but looking at other women around me who

are ageing better, staying trimmer, and always looking bright-and-breezy! I feel my friends must look at me and feel sorry for me because of how old and haggard I look these days. It's not a nice feeling."

Have you ever felt envious of someone else's looks, or despaired of your own? Have you ever been relieved and a little proud of how you haven't let yourself go like someone else, or noticed that you've kept up with this year's fashions better than someone else? That's probably caused by image-triggered CCS.

And in the western world, this trigger is everywhere. A large part of the advertising industry is deliberately aiming to make us suffer from looking-up comparison, so that we'll buy their product, the one which (really will) give us the look they tell us we need to have if we're to feel significant, enjoy satisfaction, know security. CCS is triggered constantly by magazines, TV and adverts, as well as the other women we see each day. We either don't have "the look", and so we chase it; or we do have it, and then start fighting a losing battle with the ageing process.

It works the other way, too. We might be, or seek to become, people who don't "do" image: people who aren't as hung up on their looks, who don't spend as much on hair cuts, beauty products or designer labels as those around them. There's a slight sense of superiority that we haven't been taken in by the advertising industry in the way others have. And that sense of superiority indicates that image hasn't stopped triggering our CCS: it's just triggered a looking-down comparison, instead of a looking-up one.

Circumstances

As with the beauty industry, the whole aim of lifestyle media and advertising is to point you to some dream scenario—where you live, what you drive, where you holiday, who you're married to/going out with—and leave you dissatisfied with your life as you compare it to this perfect ideal. Then, of course, you'll need to dip into your bank account to buy the life that CCS has just promised you.

But of course, it's not just the adverts that do this to us. We all know what it is to envy those higher up the privilege scale. If only we had her house… her health… her husband.

And it's just as easy for circumstances to trigger looking-down comparisons in us. Have you ever felt pleased that you've avoided someone else's mistakes? Or thought, deep down, that you've done something to deserve your husband or your house? And have you ever found that those feelings produce a brittle insecurity—so you sometimes lie awake at night worrying about losing a circumstance you rely on to give you your security, or satisfaction?

At this point, it's worth saying that there's a difference between struggling with difficult circumstances and hoping and praying that they'll change, and having circumstance-triggered CCS. I certainly don't want to trivialise a really hard time you're going through, or sound as if I'm condemning your desire to make things better. So, what is CCS, and what isn't?

Authentic CCS: CCS is all about ranking ourselves against others, either below them (looking up to) or above (looking down on) them. Authentic looking-up CCS means you'd feel better if everyone else (or the person you're comparing yourself with) were in the same boat as you. And authentic looking-down CCS means you'd feel considerably worse if everyone else were doing as well as you.

Not CCS: Sometimes, we go through a circumstance which we hate, and wouldn't wish on anyone. In other words, our feelings are triggered by the circumstance itself, and not by comparing our circumstance with other people's. That's not CCS.

Achievements

If image is based on what we're like, and circumstances on what we have, another trigger is what we can do, or have done. Our workplace successes; qualifications; popularity; hospitality; musical abilities; things we've experienced or places we've seen; how we're raising our children, and how successful (or not) they are; and so on—all can be CCS triggers.

The workplace is full of CCS triggers. Most of us will have felt resentful or envious of a co-worker's promotion, pay-rise or praise. Perhaps we felt despairing of ourselves when we compared our abilities to theirs. Or we convinced ourselves that they just got lucky, and began to feel bitter that their "luck" hadn't been given to us.

And many of us will have felt proud about working more extra hours than someone else. Or superior to the person who simply cannot get their head round the computer system. Or entitled to an extra ten minutes at lunch, because it was our pitch that won the contract.

If, on the other hand, you're a stay-at-home mum, the triggers will be different. Are your CCS symptoms prompted by someone else's cooking or creative abilities? Or their ability to keep their house running smoothly, hold down a part-time job, look after their elderly parents, and still look great every day? Or by someone else who is never on time, has let themselves go a little, and who lets their children run riot?

Goodness

You may have read the triggers above and felt quite relaxed. You don't struggle with your image, because you know it's what's inside that counts. Wealth and holidays and so on don't matter much to you. And you're happy with the truth that some can do more, and some less, than you: what matters is that you do your best with what you've got.

What you value is character: kindness, thoughtfulness, patience, obeying the law, and so on—what we might call "goodness".

On my better days, I'm this person. So it really stings to realise… these are all CCS triggers too! For instance, I sometimes think: "Yes, that family have nicer holidays than mine do, but they're basically selfish. They spend all their money and time on themselves. We're investing in others' lives; that's what really counts."

I've simply started comparing our "goodness" with theirs. And I'm coming off better! I'm not looking up at their circumstances; but I am looking down at their goodness.

Christian-ness

If you're reading this and you're not a Christian, you might think that my point is that Christians are better than this. If you are a Christian, you might be thinking: "I know that it's not about image. That circumstances aren't important. That my achievements are God-given. That I'm not good enough for God, so there's no point in being proud."

It could seem that CCS doesn't apply to Christians; but in fact it does. The symptoms are the same, it's just that living as a Christian introduces a whole new set of triggers.

> *"I am a good musician, and I love being part of the music ministry at church. Well, I love it except the times when someone new joins who quickly proves better than me at playing or singing. Then I want to pull out of doing it, because I don't want to look second-rate next to them. I envy their abilities; and I get resentful that they're better. Normally, instead of pulling out, I actually just practise more during the week, to make sure I'm as good."*

> *"Sometimes, when I listen to someone else reading the Bible in church, I feel a bit smug. I know I read it better than they do, and I find myself thinking that they should really practise more beforehand, or else not be asked at all. So I'm always pleased to be asked to read, because I know I'll do it better."*

This is CCS with a Christian veneer. It looks really great—singing well as part of the music group, or reading well at the front of church—but in fact, it's moving the goalposts while playing the same game.

And these are just two Christian-ness triggers. If you're a Christian, have you ever caught yourself thinking:

- *I know my Bible much better than they do / I'll never remember as many Bible verses as they do?*

- *I would never commit that sin like they do / I keep on sinning so much more than everyone else?*
- *I do so much more for our church than others do / I don't have anything to contribute to my church?*
- *I have given up so much more than other people in order to live as a Christian / I'm useless at this Christian life, everyone else is so much better than me?*

In thinking these things, we look up at those who are "better" Christians, and feel despair or envy. We grow bitter with God for changing, helping or using others more than us. Or, we look down on others who are not such "good" Christians as us, feel proud of our own efforts and talents, and suspect that God is fortunate to have us as His follower, and that He owes us. It's CCS.

Like the "goodness" triggers, these triggers appear less "worldly" than others— but it's the same syndrome with the same symptoms. It's just that superficially, it's Christian-looking. I find it harder to spot, and easier to hide from or make excuses for.

And, just like all other bouts of CCS, it has a serious effect on us, and on those around us.

OUTLOOK

CCS is a damaging syndrome, not just in terms of our feelings, but also when it comes to our relationships. In both the short-term and the long-term, the outlook for CCS strugglers is not good.

My relationship with myself

Have you ever met someone who projects a great air of confidence, and yet at the same time seems radically insecure? Who comes across as pretty impressive no matter what the topic of conversation—who's always the funniest, or the highest-achieving, or the most experienced? It's pretty intimidating!

One of the things I find most unsettling, but also liberating, about the Bible is that it tackles the heart head on, and calls things for what they are. And what I've called "a great air of confidence", God simply calls "arrogance"; a desire to be self-sufficient. And He describes people who are "arrogant and never at rest ... never satisfied" (Habakkuk 2 v 5).

Perhaps you are someone who feels the need always to be better—and, let's be honest, it's exhausting. Your view of yourself becomes incredibly brittle. You struggle to admit to yourself that someone does something better than you, because that undermines your whole self-image and your sense of significance. Your identity is based on the idea that you are better than others, though of course you don't put it like that. CCS has left you proud, and insecure about who you are.

On the other hand—and this is the more common feeling in women, I think—CCS can leave us hating ourselves. We see who others are, or at least we see how others project themselves to us, and we despair of who we are in comparison. We long to be like them. The Bible puts it poetically:

> *A heart at peace gives life to the body, but envy rots*
> *the bones.*   *(Proverbs 14 v 30)*

Looking-up comparison leaves us thoroughly dissatisfied with who we are; crushed in our self-perception of our abilities and characteristics. We can't accept who we are until we meet some standard that we set by comparing ourselves with others. Down this road lies chronic under-confidence.

Often, we're a mixture of the two—looking up and looking down. I recently heard a model confess on TV that she thinks models are among the most insecure women of all. Why? Because they are continually being compared with others, and comparing themselves with others. Their whole job depends on comparing favourably. And even though they come off better than most women when it comes to beauty, there will always be another model to look up at; and there will always be the nagging knowledge that beauty tends to fade! High cheekbones do not guarantee a heart of peace—quite the opposite.

The brittle or despairing self-image that CCS causes is quite neatly encapsulated in the novel *Warnings and Gales,* by Annie Sanders. Two women—the competent but slightly frumpy housewife, Imogen, and the feisty, sexy, single mum and doctor Jo—have ended up on holiday together. Towards the end of the book, they admit to each other how they feel about one another:

Jo said, "I know it's a bit late in the day, but I might as well admit it. Right from the word go, I've felt really envious of the way you make it all look so easy. One minute you're whipping up hot chocolate, the next it's wipes and plasters in your handbag—not to mention the cooking. You can even do the Heimlich manoeuvre better than me."

Imogen smiled a little. "I did a course. You can't…"

"…Be too careful?" Jo laughed. "It's just really intimidating being with someone as competent as you." Jo sat back, feeling strangely relieved to have off-loaded all that. But Imogen was staring at her, frowning. Had she said too much again?

"What? Me? Intimidating? Jo, I've felt intimidated by you from the moment you got here." Jo was stunned. "Well, look at you. You're slim, you wear fantastic clothes, you always look gorgeous, men stare at you wherever we go, you've got a great career… Next to you, I feel like a boring, lumpy, frowsy old bag!"

Jo mirrored the puzzlement and disbelief on Imogen's face, then a low chuckle rose from her throat and she shook her head slowly. "What have we been doing to each other? This was supposed to be a holiday, not a form of torture."¹

Remember that comparison was meant to show us that we're significant and satisfied and secure? Instead, it steals our joy.

My relationship with others

One of the most depressing truths about suffering from CCS is that it stops us loving others.

The Bible is full of warning stories which are essentially examples of CCS run riot. Take the historical story of Joseph and his brothers, for instance. Joseph's father, Jacob (also called Israel) "loved Joseph more than any of his [eleven] other sons" (Genesis 37 v 3). And to show this, he gave Joseph, and only Joseph, "an ornate robe".

How did his brothers respond? When they "saw that their father loved him more than any of them, they hated him" (v 4). They compared themselves with Joseph on the basis of their father's love, came off worse, and were filled with envious hatred.

How did Joseph respond? He shared his dreams with them: "We were binding sheaves of corn out in the field when suddenly my sheaf rose and stood upright, while your sheaves gathered round mine and bowed down to it" (v 7).

Why did Joseph choose to share his dream in which he ruled his older brothers? Maybe he was simply young and naïve. But probably he wanted them to know that, compared to them, he was greater, more successful, and headed for more significance than them. While his brothers show the symptoms of looking-up comparison, he displays the symptoms of looking-down comparison.

It all ended in tears, of course (though God, wonderfully, was working to bring good out of it in the end). One day, Joseph was sent by his father to find his brothers, who were tending sheep miles away. As Joseph, wearing his special cloak, approached (v 23), the brothers decided to take him down a peg or two: "Let's kill him … then we'll see what comes of his dreams" (v 20). CCS had produced a tinderbox of pride and envy, which now exploded into conspiracy to murder. In the end, they settled for selling Joseph as a slave to some foreigners, and lying to their father about what had happened to him (v 31-33).

Resentment is the by-product of envy. If we compare and come off worse, we resent those who seem to have it better. When something great happens to a friend, we can't feel happy for them. We're too busy feeling envious of them, and sad for ourselves. We're too wrapped up in thinking: "It's just so unfair".

> *"When my husband and I were struggling to have children, I found it almost impossible to be genuinely happy for friends who were 'popping out' numbers two, three or four. At one point I couldn't even bring myself to go to baby showers. I didn't want to hand over a gift or say congratulations. I tried to steer clear of people with children. I know other women who don't have children and who were able to be happy for others, but for me there could be no real rejoicing."*

If we've built our sense of significance as a person on being part of a group of friends… or if our security comes from being wealthier than those around us… then a change in other people's circumstances threatens our whole sense of who we are. If a new girl joins the church and is one of those people who draws friends like bees to a honeypot… or if a friend inherits a fortune from that rich, elderly aunt that everyone other than us seems to have… we resent them. We had been able to proudly look down in those areas; now suddenly we feel the envy of looking up. We wish they weren't around us; or we try to make sure that we're not around them.

What the brothers' envious resentment drove them to was pretty extreme. I imagine CCS has never prompted you to plot murder or sell a sibling into slavery! But what CCS feelings do cause us to do is to seek to make someone else's life worse.

Have you ever found yourself gossiping or making negative comments about someone whose popularity you're secretly a little envious of? Why do we do that? Because we want to drag them down a notch or two in front of others, so that we can more easily match up to them. The feeling of envy produced by CCS has turned itself into the action of gossip. Though we don't want to be known as a gossip, CCS turns us into one. And, when we realise this, what do we do? Either we realise we're much less nice compared to others, and here comes more despair, self-hate, and guilt. Or we just find someone who is more of a gossip compared to us, and here comes the pride and superiority!

In the end, CCS even stops us loving our loved ones. CCS makes life all about me; about me managing to match up, or stay ahead. When I do things for them, it's so that I compare favourably with others. When I encourage them to change, it's so that I'll look like a better daughter, wife, mother, or older Christian friend/adviser. When they make a mistake, I may well be more irritated about how that reflects on me than I am sad for them. It looks like I'm doing it all for them; actually, it's all for me.

It's worth pausing here and asking ourselves:

- *Are there ways I try to bring others down a peg or two, so that I can compare more favourably to them?*
- *Have I failed, underneath my smile, to celebrate good news with a friend, because deep down I'm resenting her?*
- *Are there ways I try to alter my friends or family so that I'll compare well with others, rather than acting for their sake?*
- *Do I ever become angry with my loved ones because of how their actions make me look?*

Of course, looking-down comparisons are no better for our relationships with others. A superior attitude can make us patronising, impatient, dismissive or worse to those we think of as inferior to us. And when this kind of CCS operates at a group level, its effects are multiplied. School bullying in the playground is often a group activity, because children love to feel part of an "in-crowd", superior and safer than those who are on the "outside". And in the adult world, group-level CCS leads to cultural prejudice and racism, where a group or a whole "race" seek to push others down so that they can find significance or security in being "better". Living in South Africa, it's still very easy to see the sinister effect of one people group rooting their identity in opposition to, and comparison with, another. It's CCS on a national level; and it's horrible.

When CCS gets a grip, it doesn't only steal our joy; it stops our love. And that still isn't the worst of it, because CCS also affects…

My relationship with God

Jesus once told a story about two men. It's essentially about two different ideas about how to have a relationship with God. Spot the CCS going on here:

> *¹⁰ Two men went up to the temple to pray, one a Pharisee and the other a tax collector. ¹¹ The Pharisee stood by himself and prayed: "God, I thank you that I am not like other people— robbers, evildoers, adulterers—or even like this tax collector. ¹² I fast twice a week and give a tenth of all I get."*
>
> *(Luke 18 v 10-12)*

Let's face it, in religious terms, this guy looks very, very good. He is a Pharisee: a religious leader, really strict with himself about keeping God's laws. And he is confident that he is right with God, in relationship with God, headed for heaven with God. Why? Because he's better than others.

So he thanks God "that I am not like other people" (v 11). He compares himself with those around him, and comes off very well. And you can hear the pride and superiority in his tone. CCS has told him that when it comes to God and him, all is well. He's entitled to God's friendship—after all, he's better than everyone else.

There's another man in the temple. He's a tax collector—a traitor, a cheat, the lowest of the low. Unlike the Pharisee, he...

> *stood at a distance. He would not even look up to heaven, but beat his breast and said "God, have mercy on me, a sinner". (v 13)*

To feel the force of what Jesus says next, we need to grasp who these two characters are. One is a good, moral, religious man—the first-century equivalent of a minister. The other is a selfish, amoral, exploitative man—the equivalent of a con-man who preys on old women.

But Jesus says:

> *"I tell you that this man, rather than the other, went home justified before God." (v 14)*

The conman is "justified"—in right relationship with God; the minister isn't. If that seems odd, it'll all become clear in chapter six. But the point for now is that the Pharisee wasn't justified. God rejected the man who approached Him on the basis of his comparative goodness.

And Jesus wasn't telling that story for the benefit of Pharisees: He told it "to some who were confident of their own righteousness and looked down on everyone else" (v 9). That brings it closer to home. Jesus has in His sights anyone who thinks they are fine with God because they are good enough, or moral enough, or religious enough.

That's because "enough" has to be based on a comparison. If I say I am "good enough to go to heaven", I'm saying that I am better than some other people, and so am entitled to a place in heaven. I'm looking down on some other people and saying: "God, I am not like other women—I'm not like them. I look after my family... I work hard... I don't put others down... I go to church... I don't sleep around. I'm good enough for you."

That's the looking-down CCS approach to our relationship with God. I reckon that's the view of themselves and God that most people have. It's the one I had for years. And Jesus says: it leaves you facing life without God. Be careful.

But, if we're in the grip of CCS, what's the alternative to looking down? Isn't it looking up?! It's very easy to look at those who are better, or nicer, or more "good" than us, and conclude that we have no hope of making God pleased with us. We despair at our own lack of goodness; or we grow bitter with God for setting the bar higher than we can manage; or we decide to ignore God and His standards altogether and hope that He isn't there, or won't mind.

A sense of superiority means God rejects us when we approach Him; but a sense of inferiority will mean we never approach God in the first place. It would be like that tax collector thinking: "Boy, look at that Pharisee. I've got to be that good to be in God's good books. I never fast, and I take other people's money instead of giving my own away. There's no point in even trying; God will never want me." And if he'd thought like that, he'd never have even turned up to the temple to speak to God that day.

CCS affects not only how we think we become right with God, but also how we stay right with God. That Pharisee presumably didn't get up that morning and think: "I need to get right with God". He thought he already was, and that his goodness compared to others kept him acceptable to God. The idea that God gives us a place in heaven, and then we have to do well enough to keep earning that place, is a common view among professing Christians. But again, Jesus says it doesn't work. And again, what's the alternative? To despair. To look at your Christian life and think: "I'm just not good enough. Look at how much better other Christians obey God than me. Look at how much more God won't keep wanting me in heaven. Look at how badly I'm doing."

"As a result of years of struggle with a low level of fatigue, I often feel very unproductive compared with my Christian friends. I frequently need afternoon sleeps and can't be busy many evenings in a row, or else my immunity plummets and I get sick. Until recently, I found that in the periods where I felt reasonably energetic and could keep up with others around me, I'd feel confident in my faith: that I was 'good enough'. When I felt tired and could accomplish very little, I'd look at the other women in church, and feel inadequate and concerned about my relationship with Christ. Deep down, I thought my lack of productivity meant God wouldn't be pleased with me. My relationship with God was on a roller-coaster, depending on who I spent time with and how busy and fruitful I felt in comparison with them."

Whether we look down or look up, CCS makes it all about us: about our goodness, or our lack of goodness. Either way, it ultimately destroys our relationship with God.

How seriously you take this depends on how you see God. The Bible reveals that for all of us, God is the source of everything we have that is good, including life itself (James 1 v 17; Job 12 v 10). That continues to be the case beyond death. In the life beyond this one, people in relationship with God—"justified" by Him—will enjoy only good things. Those who don't know God, on the other hand, will be left with nothing, for ever, no matter what they achieved or accumulated in this life.

That makes a lack of justification by God eternally serious. CCS steals our joy and stops us truly loving others. But most importantly of all, it can destroy the only relationship which will matter for ever: our relationship with God.

Which is why it's great news that there's a different way to approach God. The tax collector, the first-century conman, the guy who we would almost all naturally want to look down on, shows us this. He does something that leaves him, Jesus says, "justified before God" and "exalted" by God (v 14).

The great news is that Jesus cuts through CCS, taking us beyond looking up or looking down and showing that pride or despair aren't the only options. There is a way to live which allows us to be at peace with ourselves; to love others; and to enjoy life with God.

Experience contentment

The Bible calls that experience "contentment"—a life knowing real significance, satisfaction and security. It's a life where we can say what one Christian, Paul, could say: "I have learned to be content whatever the circumstances ... I have learned the secret of being content in any and every situation, whether well fed or hungry" (Philippians 4 v 11-12)—whether doing well and able to look down at others; or whether doing badly and having to look up at others.

Wouldn't that be wonderful?! To be contented with who you are, what you're doing, and where you're headed; and to have this contentment regardless of what is happening around you, regardless of your image and circumstances and achievements and goodness?

There is a way to know, to experience, to feel contentment. And it doesn't come from CCS. It comes from finding a way to live without it.

False medicines

So how can we defeat CCS? There are lots of suggested treatments—we actually hear them quite often. Here are a few I've heard, and a few that I've said to other people too, which are totally unhelpful in the long run:

- *"When you feel down, just remember all the ways in which you are attractive/gifted/successful." This is simply asking someone to replace a looking-up comparison with a looking-down comparison. It's essentially saying: Instead of thinking about something which makes you feel despair, find something which can make you feel proud for a while!*
- *"Remember, they probably have some problems in other parts of their life." If my main "trigger" is looking up at someone else's marriage, then I am going to envy them. It doesn't make any difference if they have a problem in an area that isn't a "trigger" for me.*
- *"Do something about it." This, again, is simply encouraging me to get to a position where I can swap "looking up" for "looking down".*
- *"There are people far worse off than you." Again, this is using looking-down comparison to treat looking-up comparison!*
- *"Accept yourself as you are." This actually means "be proud of who you are"; it will mean I either think I am good enough for God (like the Pharisee), or that I keep Him at arm's length because I don't want to accept that I'm not good enough. It will also mean I have to try to ignore my flaws and failings, because otherwise how can I accept myself? My self-image will be very brittle.*

Ultimately, none of these are much more effective than applying a sticking plaster to a broken leg. That's because none of them deals with the cause of CCS. And if you don't understand the cause of something, you can't treat it…

CAUSE

It may well be that since you've started reading this book (unless you've read it in a single sitting!), two things have happened.

First, you've noticed far more often that you're comparing yourself to someone; it's worse than you realised! In fact, you're realising just how compulsive comparison is!

Second, you've been trying not to compare. But you can't stop doing it. It's really frustrating—it is a syndrome we can't shake. Is there a cure for CCS?

Yes, there is. But to treat it, we need to know what the cause is. CCS isn't a skin-deep problem. Ultimately, it's a heart issue. The roots of CCS are in our hearts, in the motivational and emotional engine-room of our lives. So it's our hearts that we need to treat. But before we can find effective treatment, we need to be clear what the cause is. That's what this chapter is about.

Long, long ago...
CCS isn't a new thing. In fact, it's been a feature of life almost since humanity began. To see the cause of CCS, we're starting with the very first humans. They'll show us why CCS is so rooted in our hearts; and they'll show us that, wonderfully, it doesn't need to be like this...

> *27 So God created mankind in his own image, in the image of God he created them; male and female he created them.*
> *28 God blessed them and said to them, "Be fruitful and increase in number; fill the earth and subdue it. Rule over the fish in the sea and the birds in the sky and over every living creature that moves on the ground."*
> *29 Then God said, "I give you every seed-bearing plant on the face of the whole earth and every tree that has fruit with seed in it. They will be yours for food. 30 And to all the beasts of the earth and all the birds in the sky and all the creatures that move along the ground—everything that has the breath of life in it—I give every green plant for food." And it was so.*
> *31 God saw all that he had made, and it was very good. And there was evening, and there was morning—the sixth day.*
>
> *(Genesis 1 v 27-31)*

When the world was new, it was, as God Himself put it, "very good". And people—men and women—were "blessed" (v 28). Blessing isn't a word we use very often today. (Some people use it to describe a prayer before a meal, or after a church service, but that's not how the Bible uses it.) To be "blessed" is to enjoy significance, security and satisfaction in this world, without dilution, disappointment or death.

Where does this blessing come from? From the One who designed the world; from God Himself. The reason the first man and woman—Adam and Eve—enjoyed blessing was because God was at the centre of the world, and blessing comes from Him. The reason all of us look for blessing in our lives today is because we were made to experience those things, just as Adam and Eve were. And we were made to receive our significance, our security and our satisfaction by enjoying knowing God, just as they were.

Humans are made by God, and "in the image of God" (v 27). We are able to relate to God Himself, and reflect who He is to the world. That makes each and every human hugely, and equally, significant. God put you together in the womb (Psalm 139 v 13-16). He has already mapped out your life (139 v 15). He knows what you'll say before you say it (139 v 4). And He's made you to know Him.

That's a glorious, honoured position to hold. Neither a rabbit nor a rock can know God and enjoy relationship with Him. We can, because He made us in His image. Our significance does not come from which family we're born into, who we married, what we do Monday to Friday or how we serve on a Sunday. It comes from being made by God, to know God.

It's really quite mind-blowing. The One who spoke planets into being and flung stars into space thought of you, made you to be you, and loves you as you. No one can take that away from you, or give you any greater significance than that. We can never be, and never need to feel, worthless.

And humans are made to enjoy a "very good" world in relationship with its Creator (Genesis 1 v 31). The first two chapters of Genesis give us a glimpse of a world in which everything works and nothing frustrates—in which everything gives satisfaction. God told the first humans to do two things; to "be fruitful and increase in number", and to "rule" the rest of the creation (v 28).

In other words, God gave them two gifts: having families, and doing the job of looking after the world. In this "very good" world of perfect relationships between God and people, neither families nor work provoked frustration or prompted fear; both always provided fulfilment. Whether at home or at work, this was a world where humans could end every day satisfied with their place in the world, and could know they were not missing out in any way. They were God's people living according to God's design.

But neither significance nor satisfaction in life can be fully enjoyed if they can be lost; we can't enjoy 100% today what we know we might lose tomorrow. What was wonderful about the way God designed humans to live was that He gave them complete security. In the centre of the wonderful garden that He gave Adam and Eve to live in were two trees—the "tree of life" and the "tree of the knowledge of good and evil" (2 v 9). And God told them they could eat from the first, but not from the second (v 16-17). Both the eating and the not-eating were wonderful. Because they could eat from the tree of life, these humans knew the security of being free from the fear of death. They could enjoy life in this world every day, knowing that it could not be their last. And because they could not eat from the second tree, which represented the power to decide right and wrong, to rule the world, they could know that God was in charge of the world and of them. They could live secure in the knowledge that they were in the safest hands possible— that God was ruling, guiding, helping them.

We were made to know significance, satisfaction and security. We were all designed to enjoy blessing in God's world from knowing and finding our sense of who we are from God our Ruler:

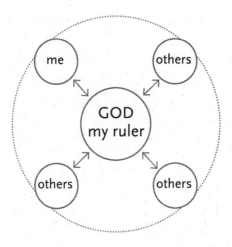

And that's exactly what the first humans experienced. So what went wrong?!

Pushing God aside

CCS is, ultimately, caused by our desire to put "me" at the centre of the universe, and at the centre of our hearts. Here's where it started:

> *¹ Now the snake was more crafty than any of the wild animals the Lord God had made. He said to the woman, "Did God really say, 'You must not eat from any tree in the garden'?"*
> *² The woman said to the snake, "We may eat fruit from the trees in the garden, ³ but God did say, 'You must not eat fruit from the tree that is in the middle of the garden, and you must not touch it, or you will die.'"*
> *⁴ "You will not certainly die," the snake said to the woman.*
> *⁵ "For God knows that when you eat from it your eyes*

*will be opened, and you will be like God, knowing good
and evil."*
*⁶ When the woman saw that the fruit of the tree was good
for food and pleasing to the eye, and also desirable for
gaining wisdom, she took some and ate it. She also gave
some to her husband, who was with her, and he ate it.*

(Genesis 3 v 1-6)

Why did the woman eat from the "tree that is in the middle of
the garden" (v 2), which God had told them not to eat from?
Because the devil (appearing to her as a serpent) convinced her
that if she took it, she would "be like God" (v 5).

The devil's lie is simple: life would be better if you got
rid of God, and became your own Ruler. You'd know more
blessing without God than you do with Him. And tragically,
the woman chose to believe him. Forgetting how wonderful
life with God as Ruler was, and forgetting that blessing was
found in knowing God, she chose to push Him out and put
herself at the centre of her life. And, when her husband saw
her doing it, he decided to do the same.

Myself at the centre

What's the first thing you do when you look at a group photo
that includes yourself? You find you, of course! We view the
world through a lens which has our own image and interests
firmly at the centre. Our first instinct when something
happens to us, or we see something new, or someone else does
something, is to ask: "How does this affect me? How does this
make me feel?" We love to be in control, to be in a privileged
position, to receive admiration. We love to take God's place.

We're at the centre. God (if we acknowledge His existence at all) is not the ultimate being—I am.

But now that I'm in the middle, how do I know I'm experiencing the best I can? How do I know I'm making a success of life? I can't find my significance, my security and satisfaction from knowing God as my Ruler—I pushed Him out of that position and seated myself in the throne.

I can only look for it in relation to others, by measuring myself up against them. I'll have to check that I'm doing better than they are. I'll have to see how they're doing better than me so I can try to get what they have.

Here's how the first woman changed her world—and how we instinctively view ours:

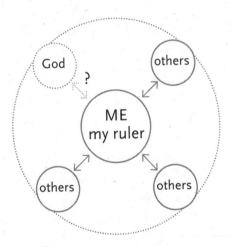

So we look at other people and think: "If I were as good at that as she is, I'd be significant—I'd be a valuable person." "If I had as much of that as they do, I'd be satisfied—I would be able to really enjoy life." "If I had that aspect of their life, then I'd be secure—I'd feel that life was under control."

The *that* could be anything; we use it to measure ourselves against others, because we think that if we have enough of it, we'll be blessed. The Bible calls these measures "idols"—things that seem to offer significance, satisfaction, security. Author and pastor Timothy Keller puts it like this:

> *"If anything becomes more fundamental than God to your happiness, meaning in life, and identity, then it is an idol"*[2].

As we compare ourselves with others on our idol measures, if we score higher then we'll look down; if we score lower, we'll look up.

How do we choose what measures to use when we compare ourselves with others? Sometimes, it's by looking at people around us to see what they think will bring them blessing, and then comparing ourselves with them on that measure:

> *"I was happy with my marriage until I heard some other women at work talking about their relationships. Their husbands sounded really romantic—and they had lots of sex! Suddenly, I felt dissatisfied with my husband. His kindness, trustworthiness and stability didn't matter anymore—now he seemed inadequate. It changed the way I thought about him; I found fault with him at every opportunity. My marriage didn't measure up, and I felt he was to blame. I wasn't going to make an effort until he became a husband as 'good' as other husbands. It was horrid."*

Knowing God wasn't where this woman looked for satisfaction; a romantic marriage had replaced Him. That was her idol-measure, given to her by her co-workers. If only her husband were as fun and romantic as her co-workers' husbands, she would be satisfied in life. Since he wasn't (or didn't seem to be), she was dissatisfied. She was trapped in CCS.

More often, though, our idol-measures are provided by our upbringing and childhood experiences:

"My family always set huge store by exam results. I grew up being taught subliminally that people with academic intelligence were 'better' than others. Since I tended to be towards the top of the class, that meant I was 'better'. Years later, I still struggle not to seek to appear cleverer than those around me, and I feel insecure and intimidated when I'm with anyone who I know is more intelligent than I am."

Being made by God, uniquely formed by Him in His image, isn't where this woman finds her sense of self-worth; in other words, her significance. Instead, intelligence is. That's her idol-measure, given to her by her family. If she has enough intelligence—if she is intelligent when compared to those around her—she feels significant. If not, all her self-worth disappears. She's trapped in CCS.

Our idol-measure can be anything. Romantic marriage and intelligence are just two. Some of us may see savings as what gives us security—and we compare our investments with those of others to see if we're really secure. Some of us need to lose weight to feel self-worth—as long as we're a bit slimmer than our friends, that will be enough. Some of us find our satisfaction in our lovely home—until someone in our neighbourhood has a beautiful extension put on theirs. None of those things are bad in themselves—it's just that we've made these good things into ultimate things.

We're so easily, and so often, trapped in compulsive comparison syndrome—and CCS is way more serious than a very common bad habit. Measuring ourselves against others, desiring a better position, is a direct result of us taking God's place at the centre of the world and looking for blessing in things that are not our Creator. The reality of CCS shows that our hearts are rejecting God's loving rule in our lives.

In a world where "I" am at the centre instead of God, CCS will be a constant companion. It has to be.

CCS unleashed

The link between rejecting God's rule ("sinning"), and losing blessing and so suffering from CCS, rapidly becomes clear as humans live in a world with themselves at the centre.

First, it shows itself in their relationship with God. When God confronts the two humans about what they've done, He asks the man: "Have you eaten from the tree from which I commanded you not to eat?" (3 v 11).

The man's response is a classic attempt to base a relationship with God on looking-down comparison: "The woman you put here—she gave me some fruit from the tree, and I ate it" (v 12). The man approaches God on this basis: "Yes I ate it. But she took it from the tree. Compared to her, I'm not that bad!"

God then turns to the woman: "What is this you have done?" And she answers: "The serpent deceived me, and I ate" (v 13). Her grounds for thinking she's OK with God are: "Yes I ate it. But the serpent was the one who tricked me.

Compared to him, I'm not that bad!" Notice that she doesn't compare herself with her husband, but with someone that is less good than her.

This is the approach to God which that Pharisee adopted in Jesus' story; finding people to look down on so that we seem comparatively "good enough" for God. As Jesus said, God does not accept the proud. And the next time God speaks to the first man and woman, it's to banish them from the garden and from His presence and blessing.

CCS ruins people's relationship with God; it also wrecks their relationship with each other. Eve had two children: Cain and Abel. When they both brought offerings to God, God was pleased with Abel's, but not with Cain's (Genesis 4 v 4-5). We're not really told why; that's not the point. What matters is how Cain responds.

"Cain was very angry" (v 5): he compared himself with his brother and came off worst. He was envious of his brother's acceptance, and he was bitter towards the God who had not given him what he wanted.

And his feelings led to actions: "Cain attacked his brother Abel and killed him" (v 8). It's only a generation since humanity was enjoying eternal life; now one human ends the life of another.

Fast forward through the millennia, and CCS is simply a part of our lives. Here's how the Bible describes humanity throughout the ages. It doesn't make for pleasant reading but, if we're honest, it does make for an accurate summary:

> [29] *They have become filled with every kind of wickedness,*
> *evil, greed and depravity. They are full of envy, murder, strife,*
> *deceit and malice. They are gossips,* [30] *slanderers, God-haters,*

> *insolent, arrogant and boastful; they invent ways of doing*
> *evil; they disobey their parents;* [31] *they have no understanding,*
> *no fidelity, no love, no mercy.*   *(Romans 1 v 29-31)*

Did you notice how many of those descriptions of humans were feelings that are symptoms of CCS (envy, arrogance, boastfulness ie: superiority) or the actions that those feelings become (murder, strife, deceit and malice, gossip, slander, faithlessness)? Not all sin is a result of CCS; but all CCS is, at root, sin—a result of pushing God out of the centre so that we can rule our own lives and seek our blessings elsewhere.

Broken cisterns

We've already seen that a life spent seeking blessing through comparison doesn't deliver. Now, we can see why it doesn't deliver—and why it never will.

It's because, as Romans 1 puts it neatly, people did not, and do not, "think it worth while to retain the knowledge of God, [and so] he gave them over to a depraved mind, to do what ought not to be done" (v 28).

We each choose not to treat God as God, not to know Him as our Ruler. So He allows us to have what we've chosen; minds and hearts which seek blessing elsewhere. And He allows us to act as we have chosen—to do the things which searching for blessing elsewhere produces in our efforts to gain or keep that blessing.

But God created a world in which we could and would find significance, satisfaction and security from knowing Him; in relationship with Him, living under His rule. Blessing isn't found anywhere else. God gives us a helpful image to describe what we've done:

> *People … have forsaken me, the spring of living water, and*
> *have dug their own cisterns, broken cisterns that cannot hold*
> *water.*   *(Jeremiah 2 v 13)*

We could have known blessing from God. But we've chosen to look elsewhere for significance, satisfaction, or security. Those things weren't designed to deliver them; and God won't let them.

We were made to know "the spring of living water"—God; created to enjoy His blessing and to overflow it to each other and the world. Pushing God out of our lives and making ourselves our own ruler doesn't stop us being human. But it does mean we've cut ourselves off from the only source of blessing. We go on living, yet we are so much less than the people we could be, should be, were made to be. And one day, we'll leave all our successes behind anyway.

Of course, we still live in a world which was made to be "very good"; and we see very good reflections of that original, wonderful creation all around us, and in our own lives. But blessing proves elusive. Wherever we seek it, chase it, and even seem to grasp it, it slips away.

After leaving home, I lived in a shared flat for just over a decade before I got married. All that time, I longed to have "my own home" which I could decorate and buy stuff for; a house like some of my friends who were getting married lived in. But after my wedding, we lived in a small, rented one-bedroom flat. I carried on dreaming of getting my own big house, and envying those who did. If I just had that kind of house, I imagined, my messiness would sort itself out, I'd love coming home, and I'd feel settled and secure about life.

We got that kind of house, eventually. It was great—but it wasn't what I'd pictured. The messiness continued (it just had more space to spread out in!). The decorating proved very stressful and then mildly disappointing, or just didn't happen at all. It was a lovely house—but after a while, I realised it wasn't going to give me all that I thought it would. After all, it was only a house.

We know what it is to compare ourselves with someone, fall short, and conclude that we need more of what they have—surely then we'll feel blessed. We know what it is to wonder if we've been chasing the wrong thing, and switch our efforts to gaining something else instead—surely then we'll feel blessed. And we know what it is to make huge sacrifices to finally grab what we thought would give us blessing—only to find that what we'd craved doesn't deliver all that it promised, for as long as it promised. So we look for more of it, more of something else, or give up and despair.

In other words, our experience of life confirms to us that God's words are true. We dig our own cisterns, and we make a rubbish job of it. They're cracked, and no matter what we seek to fill our lives with, blessing drains away.

But since God's words are true, there is a spring of living water. There is a treatment for CCS…

TREATMENT

In the end, the treatment for CCS is wonderfully, challengingly simple. The medicine can be summed up in a few words:

Let God be God.

Our compulsive need to compare comes from pushing God out of the centre; as does our forlorn and futile search for blessings. So the cure is simply to reverse the way we see the world, and ourselves. We need to restore God to the centre of our lives, and to find all we need, at each point of our days and in every part of our dreams, in Him.

Let God be God. If ever something was easier said than done, it is that! It's not difficult to understand the truths that we're looking at in this chapter, and to know that God should be God in our lives. But to actually live as though God is God, so that our blessings are all found in Him... that's a very different thing. I'm aware that I often walk around knowing in my head that God is the source of blessing; but I leave that package of knowledge just there, in my head. I don't apply it to my heart. I don't trust it. I don't let it shape my life.

So it may be that you're reading this book and you're well aware that you haven't got your head around what Christianity is (in which case, read on—this chapter contains its core message). But it could also be that you're reading as someone who has all these things worked out in your understanding; but you haven't wrapped your heart around them.

The truth about God—the gospel message—is something we need to know not only intellectually, but also emotionally.

So where do we start in letting God be God? By remembering and knowing and living out two key truths about Him: that God is the blessing-bringing Creator, and that He is the blessing-restoring Saviour.

1. The blessing-bringing Creator

Remembering that God is our Creator means that we will find our confidence in who we are, what we're doing, and where we're heading through knowing Him, rather than through comparing ourselves with others.

Have a read of Psalm 8, written 3,000 years ago by the Old Testament king of Israel, David. See if you can pick out from this song where he is finding his sense of significance, satisfaction in life, and security for his present and his future.

> *¹ LORD, our Lord,*
>> *how majestic is your name in all the earth!*
> *You have set your glory*
>> *in the heavens.*
> *² Through the praise of children and infants*
>> *you have established a stronghold against your enemies,*

> to silence the foe and the avenger.
> [3] When I consider your heavens,
>   the work of your fingers,
> the moon and the stars,
>   which you have set in place,
> [4] what is mankind that you are mindful of them,
>   human beings that you care for them?
> [5] You have made them a little lower than the angels
>   and crowned them with glory and honour.
> [6] You made them rulers over the works of your hands;
>   you put everything under their feet:
> [7] all flocks and herds,
>   and the animals of the wild,
> [8] the birds in the sky,
>   and the fish in the sea,
>   all that swim the paths of the seas.
> [9] LORD, our Lord,
>   how majestic is your name in all the earth!   (Psalm 8)

David is simply doing what Adam and Eve did until they listened to the serpent; he is remembering that God is His Creator, His Ruler. And so he enjoys the significance, in a vast cosmos, of knowing that when it comes to humans "you have made them ... and crowned them with glory and honour" (v 5)—he knows he's made in God's image.

He enjoys the satisfaction of being able to say to God that "you care for" me (v 4); of knowing that God loves and looks after him. In another psalm, David encourages people to "taste and see that the Lord is good; blessed is the man who takes refuge in him" (Psalm 34 v 8). In other words, the most satisfying thing that God gives people is... Himself! Knowing

God is what brings David ultimate, lasting satisfaction; and so, because he knows God, he's satisfied with the life God has given him, getting on with the job of looking after His world (v 6).

And thirdly, David enjoys the security of remembering that God's name is "majestic ... in all the earth" (v 1, 9). He knows God is in charge. He understands that God knows what He's doing. He rests secure in the knowledge that the One who cares for him is the One who is in charge of everything.

Seeing ourselves as we are

Psalm 8 points us to God as our blessing-giving Creator. But it also reminds us of our place. David begins his song not with "I" but "You": "You have set your glory above the heavens" (v 1). If we're to let God be God, we need to remember that we're not God. The God who made the moon and the stars (v 3)—He's the One this world is all about. He's the most important Person in the cosmos; which means that you and I are not!

And naturally, we find it difficult to remember this. As we saw in the last chapter, there's something very attractive about making ourselves our own rulers. But it's as we have a right view of God, as we put our confidence in Him, that we find ourselves living the life we're searching for. We can only see God as He truly is if we're prepared to see ourselves as we really are.

But seeing ourselves as we really are doesn't stop there. It involves not only seeing that God is God, and we're not; it means accepting that we have lived as though we are God, and He isn't. The Bible calls it sin.

Sin is an unpopular concept in our culture, which tends to

tell us that the answer to our problems and worries is to build ourselves up, think better of ourselves, and love ourselves more. The Bible does the opposite: it shows us that we're worse than we like to think, that we are not lovely in any way:

> *¹ As for you, you were dead in your transgressions and sins, ² in which you used to live when you followed the ways of this world and of the ruler of the kingdom of the air, the spirit who is now at work in those who are disobedient. ³ All of us also lived among them at one time, gratifying the cravings of our flesh and following its desires and thoughts. Like the rest, we were by nature deserving of wrath. ⁴ But…*   *(Ephesians 2 v 1-4)*

I don't like to think of myself as God does! I'd far rather listen to the world telling me that I'm OK really—yes, I make some mistakes, but I'm basically fine. It's far easier to think of myself like that than as someone who is "by nature deserving of wrath" (v 3)—of God's punishment beyond death, of eternity without any blessing at all.

But, if I'm honest, God's way of looking at me, my life, and my contribution to this world is far more accurate than mine. We've already seen that we push God out of the centre, which causes our CCS. We've seen the ugly symptoms that CCS produces. When I look honestly at my own heart, at the pride and envy and anger and bitterness that live there, I begin to see that I am truly what God says I am: a sinner. Just as that tax collector, when he spoke to God, called himself simply "a sinner" (Luke 18 v 13), that's the description which best sums me up. A sinner, facing not God's pleasure and blessing but God's punishment and anger. Someone who could have known blessing in God's world by living with Him as my Creator, but who has chosen not to and has forfeited all blessing, for all time.

That's the reality. It's very depressing. But at least it's real. And in that sense, it's liberating to know that I'm a sinner. It means I don't need to pretend, to make such an effort hiding my flaws and excusing my failings. I can be honest about who I am, with myself and with God. And I can begin to appreciate the last word of the Bible passage on the previous page. "But."

Verses 1-3 are all about what we have done—sinned—and where it has got us—deserving God's eternal punishment. But… that is not the last word. God has done something to restore our lost blessing.

2. The blessing-restoring Saviour

> *⁴ But because of his great love for us, God, who is rich in mercy, ⁵ made us alive with Christ even when we were dead in transgressions—it is by grace you have been saved. ⁶ And God raised us up with Christ and seated us with him in the heavenly realms in Christ Jesus, ⁷ in order that in the coming ages he might show the incomparable riches of his grace, expressed in his kindness to us in Christ Jesus. ⁸ For it is by grace you have been saved, through faith—and this is not from yourselves, it is the gift of God—⁹ not by works, so that no one can boast. ¹⁰ For we are God's handiwork, created in Christ Jesus to do good works, which God prepared in advance for us to do.*   *(Ephesians 2 v 4-10)*

If God were only our Creator, then as sinners we'd have only two options. We could hide from our true selves, and use

CCS to find some people to look down on, and think that we deserve blessing, eternally; we could be proud, self-sufficient, entitled, and not justified, not right with God. Or we could accept that we're sinners, and despair.

Which is why letting God be God means asking Him to be our Saviour, as well as remembering that He is our Creator. Just as Psalm 8 is really about God, and not David, so Ephesians 2 is really about Jesus, not us. It's pointing us to the truth that God has made His Son the Ruler of the cosmos (the "Christ"); which means that it's in making Christ Jesus the centre of our lives that we can have our blessings restored. We don't grasp blessing for ourselves; it is given to us by Him.

Significance

God "made us alive with Christ even when we were dead in transgressions" (v 5). That's how significant you are: God loves you enough not to leave you facing His punishment. In Christ, He came and lived and died and rose as a man so that you could be made alive.

That's how loved you are; how valuable you are. No one can love us any better, any more, than the Lord Jesus, who gave up heaven and experienced hell for His people. "This is love: not that we loved God, but that he loved us and sent his Son as an atoning sacrifice for our sins" (1 John 4 v 10). The Father sent the Son, and the Son willingly died on a cross, so that the punishment for our sin could fall on Him, and the blessings that He deserves could be given to us. It's Jesus' death that enables God to look at a sinner like that tax collector and say: You are justified, you are at one with me, you will enjoy life with me. The cross is the ultimate proof that God is a God who loves. This is love: that God loves His people enough to die for them. The definition of love is the crucifixion of Christ.

If you are trusting Jesus, that's the value God places on your head, simply "because of his great love" (Ephesians 2 v 4). It's not image, circumstances or achievements that make us valuable. It's God choosing to love us. And He loves you enough to have made you part of His people and give you blessings with Him for ever.

Satisfaction

And not only has God given you eternal life, He's given you work to do throughout that life. By saving us, He has "created" us "to do good works, which God prepared in advance for us to do" (v 10). Each day, someone who has Jesus as their Saviour can know that God has useful work for them to do; a part to play in His eternal plan for this world. And they can know that they are just where they need to be, with the life that's best for them to have. They are not missing out in any way; in fact, they're part of the only work that will last for ever.

This changes how I look at life. When I wash the dishes for the umpteenth time that day... when I drop my plans for a relaxing evening to comfort a friend... when I give up buying a top because someone else needs that money more... when I remain patient in the face of a (very) trying son or daughter... these are not just random, tiring, mildly annoying parts of my day. They are good works, which God designed specifically for me to do. They are part of a plan which I can't see, but that He's working out—a plan which is of eternal importance.

But that's not the best of it. The best is yet to come, because in the future God will "show the incomparable riches of his grace" (v 7). He has saved His people for a future that is far, far better than any blessing we know in this life. He's saved us for a new world which has nothing dissatisfying in it; even the best of this world is only a faint glimmer of that one.

Security

And how do we know we'll be there? "God raised us up with Christ and seated us with him in the heavenly realms" (v 6). In a sense, when Jesus was raised from the dead 2,000 years ago, and returned to heaven, so was everyone who would trust in Him.

It's as if when He reached heaven, Jesus reserved a seat at a table for each one of His people. So there's already a chair with a name card on it that says: "Sophie de Witt". The Christian's future is completely secure, because God has secured it. The God who made the stars is quite capable of getting His people to His heaven! We are "shielded by God's power" until we reach our heavenly home (1 Peter 1 v 4), led each day along a path laid out by the One who called Himself the "good shepherd" (John 10 v 14). We are guided daily, and we are safe eternally. That's the biggest answer to all our worries about our lives and our future.

And so the treatment for CCS is to let God be God, with Christ at the centre. As we do that, we find the significance, satisfaction and security for which our hearts yearn, for which we were made, and for which the world is searching elsewhere. We know that we are made by God, and rescued by God; we can experience living God's way in God's world now as we head for His perfect future world; and we can enjoy knowing that we are cared for by the God who has already secured our eternal perfect future.

Instead of making ourselves "god" and seeing ourselves in comparison with other people, we need to see ourselves the way that, if we put our faith in Christ, God sees us:

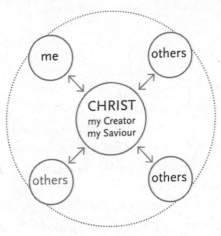

From here to heaven

The beginning of the Bible shows us a "very good" garden, a blessed past which humanity lost by sinning. The end of the Bible presents a vision of a perfect city, a blessed future which Christ offers:

[1] Then the angel showed me the river of the water of life, as clear as crystal, flowing from the throne of God and of the Lamb [2] down the middle of the great street of the city. On each side of the river stood the tree of life, bearing twelve crops of fruit, yielding its fruit every month. And the leaves of the tree are for the healing of the nations. [3] No longer will there be any curse. The throne of God and of the Lamb will be in

*the city, and his servants will serve him. ⁴ They will see his
face, and his name will be on their foreheads. ⁵ There will be
no more night. They will not need the light of a lamp or the
light of the sun, for the Lord God will give them light. And
they will reign for ever and ever.   (Revelation 22 v 1-5)*

The language here is highly symbolic, but it's describing a
concrete future reality—a place of blessings restored. People
who live in this city enjoy the significance of being God's
people, in His image—"his name will be on their foreheads"
(v 4). They will enjoy the satisfaction of reigning over the world
(v 5)—the satisfaction of living the life they were designed for.
And they'll enjoy the security of eating from "the tree of life"
(v 2)—of knowing that they can live there for ever.

Behind the symbolism is the message: This is the place you
long for, you search for, you strive for. This is the place of the
blessing you were created to experience. And in its centre is the
blessing-giver: "the Lamb", Jesus, God's Son, who died like a
lamb and rose again so that He could give people a place in
this city. There, He doesn't give just a spring of living water,
but a whole river!

This is what people who have remembered God is their
Creator, and ask Him to be their Saviour, are looking forward
to. The blessings we enjoy today by letting God be God, by
living with Christ at the centre of life, are wonderful; the
blessings we'll enjoy in the future, in heaven, are unimaginable.

From head to heart
As we walk towards that "river of the water of life", we can
drink deeply from that "spring of living water". But between

here and heaven, that's going to be a daily struggle. Even if we understand, in our heads, the facts about who God is, and what God has given us, it takes a revolution in our thinking, and our feeling, to let God actually be God in our lives. If you're a Christian, it's likely that you're frustrated by your inability to do this. The distance between our heads and our hearts seems unbridgeable!

And it is, if we try to do it on our own, or expect it to happen overnight. It is not the case that being a Christian means we don't or can't struggle with CCS. Being a Christian means that we can experience the blessing of knowing Christ today; but it doesn't mean that we always will, because it needs us to apply what we know in our heads to our hearts. It requires us to live today as though what we know is true really is true.

It takes time, and it needs outside assistance. We have to let God help us let God be God. Again, we need to see ourselves as we really are. We are not God. We are sinners. And we're unable to live with God as God without His help!

That's why God has given us His Spirit. God the Spirit is the gift of God the Father to everyone who has asked God the Son to save them. In fact, it's only through the Holy Spirit's work that we're able to understand who God is in the first place (1 Corinthians 12 v 3). And then it's only through the Spirit's work that any of us are able to live with Him as God, seeing life from His perspective, and enjoying blessing from Him:

> [11] *No-one knows the thoughts of God except the Spirit of God.*
> [12] *What we have received is not the spirit of the world, but the Spirit who is from God, so that we may understand what God has freely given us …* [15] *The person with the Spirit makes*

> *judgments about all things, but such a person is not subject to*
> *merely human judgments.*   *(1 Corinthians 2 v 11-12, 15)*

"What God has freely given us" is, supremely, His Son Jesus. It's in knowing Him that we find blessing. Jesus is God's amazing gift to you and me. He is the treatment for our CCS. But we need to apply that treatment. And that's what the Holy Spirit does for us. We are given the Spirit "so that we may understand" what is already ours. He makes it possible for us to experience— to live out and enjoy—all that Jesus has given us.

The Spirit is the doctor who applies the gospel medicine to our lives.

Perhaps you are a Christian. You have been for years. You know the gospel—you know that Jesus is your Creator and your Saviour. You know you're headed for heaven. This chapter hasn't told you anything you didn't already know. And yet CCS is a constant part of your life. You know despair, or pride, or both. Envy is your constant companion, except when you're feeling superior. You'd love to enjoy the blessings knowing Jesus brings; but you don't. How can you change?

You can't! But the Holy Spirit can change you. He will teach you to "make judgments about all things"—to see through the lies which say that image, or circumstances, or achievements, or goodness, or even Christian living itself can bring you significance, satisfaction or security. He will enable you not to worry about "merely human judgments" from those around you. He will apply to your heart, step by step, what your head already knows—He'll change your desires as well as your understanding.

What do you and I need to do? "Keep in step with the Spirit" (Galatians 5 v 25). Ask God to set His Spirit to work.

Look for His leading in your life; listen to His promptings; let Him loosen your attachment to your idol-measures. Love Him as He helps you to appreciate, to treasure, and to enjoy the blessings that are already yours in Jesus.

We need to make each CCS trigger-event a fresh opportunity to find our significance, satisfaction and security in being created by God and saved by God; a fresh opportunity to live with Christ at the centre in our heads and in our hearts. And we are able to make each failure, each time we give in to CCS, a moment where we say to God: "Have mercy on me, a sinner" (Luke 18 v 13), and know that because of what Jesus has done, He will.

Perhaps you're not a Christian, but you know you struggle with CCS, and you'd love not to. God is offering you all the significance, satisfaction and security you're looking for. Let Him be your God. You can tell Him you know He's your Creator, and ask Him to be your Saviour, and ask His Spirit to go to work in you; and then you can know real, lasting blessing, and know that nothing—not even death—can take it away from you. And if this is something you know you need to find out more about, there are a few suggestions on page 107.

HEALTHY  LIVING

One of the tragic everyday sights when living in South Africa is the beggars. They approach you at traffic lights, hoping for some spare change, which will get them their next meal; and then they're back again, begging for a little more. We see them on "rubbish day" each week, scrabbling through the rubbish for something of value.

But just imagine that one day, one of them was handed a cheque for 100 million rand (£7 million, or $12 million). They wouldn't be sitting on the roadside the next day! They'd be opening a bank account, paying the cheque in, and enjoying the money. And if a fellow beggar pointed out they were missing out on some spare change, they wouldn't mind. They'd have been given unimaginable riches. The spare change would have lost its value. Instead of scrabbling, when they needed money they'd simply visit an ATM.

God has, Paul wrote to some first-century Christians, "blessed us in the heavenly realms with every spiritual blessing in Christ" (Ephesians 1 v 3). "Every" is a pretty normal, everyday word; it's also a seriously exciting word in that sentence! Every blessing any of us need—all the significance, satisfaction and security that we were made to know and which everyone is searching for—is found in knowing Jesus as our God, as our Creator and Saviour.

So there's no need to scrabble for blessings elsewhere; no need to constantly compare ourselves with others to see if we're doing well enough, or missing out; to see if we're worthwhile or useless. All the Christian needs, the Christian has.

That's why Paul is able to say:

> [12] *I have learned the secret of being content in any and every situation, whether well fed or hungry …* [13] *I can do everything through him who gives me strength.*
>
> (Philippians 4 v 12-13)

He finds all he needs in "him who gives me strength"—in Jesus Christ. Knowing Jesus, and knowing we have all we need in knowing Jesus, leads to a real, lasting, deep contentment. It means we can echo Paul and say we know the secret of being content:

- *however we look, great or not-so-great;*
- *in any and every circumstance, good or bad;*
- *regardless of our achievements, better or worse;*
- *whether we are meeting our moral standards, or failing.*

Why? Because our significance, satisfaction and security doesn't come from gaining, keeping or increasing any of those CCS triggers. Instead, it comes from Christ. Compulsive Comparison happens when we seek blessing anywhere other than in knowing Jesus—when we see our image, circumstances, achievements, goodness, or Christian performance as being who we really are. As soon as we do that, we'll lose contentment, and we'll start to compulsively compare to see if we're matching up. As long as we look only to our relationships with Jesus to give us our blessing, we'll know contentment, and we'll be able to get on with enjoying the things in our life.

So imagine that your core identity—your sense who you are, the thing or things that give you contentment—are a circle. All around this core identity is the rest of your life: what you're like, what you have, what you do. For instance, have a look at this woman:

WHAT I'M LIKE

Musical

Good health

WHAT I HAVE

WHO I AM

Significant in Christ
Satisfied in Christ
Secure in Christ

Good looks

Small house

Raise children

Reading Bible daily

WHAT I DO

This woman will be content. Her sense of significance, satisfaction and security are unshakeable and unloseable, because she finds each one of them in her relationship in Christ.

But for each one of us, it's a daily struggle to keep living, thinking and feeling this way—to stop ourselves seeking blessing by comparing what we're like, what we have or what we do with how others are doing. Our imaginary friend finds it hard, too:

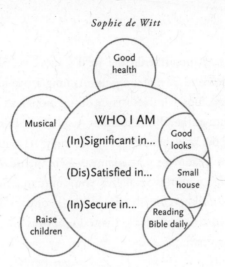

Now, she's looking to her looks, her house, and her Bible-reading habits for her sense of significance, her satisfaction, her security. Her "blessing" has become shifting and elusive—a bad hair day when going to a party, or visiting a friend's larger house, or meeting someone who reads their Bible more, and it's gone. As soon as we allow a characteristic, or circumstance, or achievement to be our blessing-giver, we'll lose blessing, start CCS, and give up contentment.

And it's only Christ-centred contentment, keeping our relationship with Him as where we find our sense of who we are, that transforms our relationships. Knowing Jesus, and knowing that we have all we need in knowing Jesus, means not that we will never compare, but that we will compare healthily, in ways which mean we love others more, not less, and enjoy blessing more, not less.

The rest of this chapter will help us see how letting God be God in our lives reverses the consequences of CCS by enabling us to compare in healthy ways in our relationships—with God, with others, and with ourselves.

My relationship with God

To imitate someone, you first need to compare yourself with them. And the Bible is full of encouragements to imitate God. Way back in the Old Testament, God called His people to be pure: "Be holy because I … am holy" (Leviticus 19 v 2). The New Testament makes the same command: "Follow God's example … and live a life of love, just as Christ loved us and gave himself up for us" (Ephesians 5 v 1-2); "Have the same mindset as Christ Jesus" (Philippians 2 v 5).

What was Jesus' attitude? The opposite of CCS. He deliberately accepted a lower position than He deserved, to serve others. Though…

> [6] *being in very nature God, [he] did not consider equality*
> *with God something to be used to his own advantage;*
> [7] *rather, he made himself nothing by taking the very nature*
> *of a servant, being made in human likeness.* [8] *And being*
> *found in appearance as a man, he humbled himself by*
> *becoming obedient to death; even death on a cross!*
>
> *(Philippians 2 v 6-8)*

And God's desire—what He's working in Christians to do—is for us to be "conformed to the likeness of His Son" (Romans 8 v 29)—to be re-made in the image of God.

If our approach to God is based on CCS, then comparing ourselves to Jesus, the perfect human, will crush us. CCS tells us that to be blessed, we need to be as good as Him. And none of us can be as perfect as the Son of God. We can only despair at ourselves and our failings; or grow bitter with God for His perfect standards; or ignore the call to be like Jesus, and settle for a standard which we make up for ourselves.

But knowing Jesus as our Creator and Saviour turns this around. It tells us that our blessing is not dependent on us matching up to Christ; it is dependent on Christ giving it to us. The gospel is not: be good enough, and Jesus will bless you. It is: the perfect Jesus has blessed you; now enjoy becoming more like Him.

I have a friend who has played tennis at international level. I can stagger around a tennis court. Imagine that our friendship rested on me matching her skill when we played together. I would hate it; it would crush me, or I would avoid playing her at all. But we're friends anyway, regardless of our relative tennis performance; and that frees me simply to enjoy playing with her. I'll never beat her, but seeing how she plays makes me a better player.

If you're not a Christian, your performance will never be good enough to secure blessing for yourself. If you are a Christian, your performance doesn't affect your blessing at all—it's already been given to you by Jesus. He "loved us and gave himself up for us"—He lived the perfect life we can't, and died the death we deserve, so that we could know Him and be blessed by Him. When a Christian succeeds in loving as Jesus would, He doesn't love or bless them any more; and when a Christian fails, He doesn't love them any less.

We'll never be as good as Jesus, but that doesn't need to make us despair or become bitter. We can simply look at Him, see how He lived, and seek to become more like Him:

> *"During the first six months of our marriage, Sarah and I fought like cats. Then one day I was reading the end of Ephesians 5, and I realised that the problem in my marriage was that I was comparing myself with Sarah,*

and thinking that I was doing better than her, and getting cross. But Ephesians 5 said I was to be a Christ-like husband, and Christ laid down His life for His people. It was as if Jesus was telling me: 'Ray, get your eyes off Sarah and onto me. When you think you have gone as far as me you can stop—until then, keep loving your woman.' That took the wind out of my sails. I was the problem! I needed to change. I needed to stop comparing how good a spouse I was with Sarah, and get on with being the Christ-like husband she needed me to be."

One sign that you're beginning to let the Spirit treat your CCS is that you take being like Christ seriously. You don't make excuses; you don't cut corners. You can compare yourself to Christ, come off worst (obviously!) and ask His Spirit to change you, all without despairing, because you know that your relationship with Him is secure.

My relationship with others

The contented Christian woman doesn't stop comparing herself with others, either! But again, the comparisons are transformed.

Christians compared with other Christians

At one point, as he writes to a struggling church, Paul tells its members to…

follow my example, as I follow the example of Christ.
(1 Corinthians 11 v 1)

To another, thriving, church, his instruction is the same:

> *Join with others in following my example, brothers, and take*
> *note of those who live according to the pattern we gave you.*
> *(Philippians 3 v 17)*

One way we become more like Jesus is by imitating other Christians who are more like Him than we are. And that's going to mean comparing ourselves with other Christians. How will we avoid looking-up comparisons and the despair or envy that accompany them; and looking-down comparisons and the pride and superiority that they prompt?

It's because we're not comparing as part of our search for blessing. If, for example, my sense of security for tomorrow and eternity rests on me obeying God really well, then seeing someone who obeys God better than I do will undermine all my security. But if my security comes from knowing that Jesus has given me a guaranteed place in heaven, then everything changes when I see someone obeying Him better than I do. I'll praise God for them. I'll pray that God would make me more like them. And I won't lose my security, because that's found in knowing the Lord Jesus and knowing that He's given me eternal life, not in obeying Him. Jesus is my blessing-giver; my obedience isn't.

On the other hand, if we see a fellow Christian struggling in some way, either spiritually or practically, we won't feel proud or superior or relieved. CCS would prompt us to look down on them; but now, we're freed to love them.

It all comes down to where we find our significance, satisfaction, or security—or what Paul labels "hope":

> *Those who are rich in this present world [should not] be*
> *arrogant nor ... put their hope in wealth, which is so*

> uncertain, but to put their hope in God, who provides us with
> everything for our enjoyment.   *(1 Timothy 6 v 17)*

If our security is in God, then Paul says we will be "generous and willing to share" our money (v 18) and everything else— time, and emotional energy, and friendship groups, and so on. We won't need to hang onto these things to enable ourselves to feel blessed as we wallow in looking-down comparison.

The solution to CCS is not simply to stop all comparisons. It's to find blessed contentment in Christ, and practise healthy comparison. How do we know the difference? By looking at what our comparison produces. If it's praise to God, prayer for ourselves, and prayer and practical love for others, then it's healthy. If it's envy, or despair, or pride, or any other symptom of CCS, then we're allowing something other than Christ to be what we look to for blessing.

At the moment, I'm finding myself comparing my lack of generosity and my regular bouts of impatience with other Christians who are so much more like Christ than I am. Maybe for you it's something else. Perhaps you've noticed that someone else prays more than you; or is more gentle; or better at talking to her friends about Jesus; or more content to be single or childless. Remember that in Jesus, you already have everything you will ever need. Don't think you need to be like them to be blessed. Then you'll be able to want to be like them to better serve your blessing-giver.

> *"I'm married with kids, and in my forties. One of my best*
> *friends is the same age, and single. And she's one of those*
> *people who packs an amazing amount into her days.*
> *I often look at her and feel envious of how flexible she can*

> *be—she has no children to keep fed and clean. Or I'm*
> *struck by a sense of my own inadequacy compared to all she*
> *accomplishes in her week. Or deep down I feel relief that I'm*
> *not single at 40. Or I feel all three at the same time!*
> *Sometimes, I remember to stop comparing myself with her*
> *like that, and know that my blessing and hers come from*
> *Jesus. That changes everything! I'm simply grateful to God for*
> *a friend who throws herself into His work so whole-heartedly.*
> *I'm can see her as a really good example. I pray for myself,*
> *that I'll become more like her in her passion for serving*
> *Christ. And I pray for her, that she'll find contentment in*
> *knowing Him, not in her circumstances. I think that when I*
> *stop my CCS, I become a much, much better friend!"*

It's only if we seek our blessings in Jesus that we're able to appreciate and enjoy the truth that God deliberately made us different and that He deliberately gave us different gifts. Your church is a "body"; and "the body is not made up of one part but of many … God has arranged the parts in the body, every one of them, just as he wanted them to be" (1 Corinthians 12 v 14, 18). God has given you some gifts, and others some different gifts, so that you need each other, and can help and encourage and support each other.

But CCS prevents us doing any of that—and I think CCS is rife in churches. It's damaging for church members; and it's seriously offputting to outsiders, who instead of witnessing Christian community are in fact experiencing gatherings full of pride, envy, superiority and bitterness. It will stop us enjoying both our own and others' gifts; it will tell us we have nothing to offer; and it will encourage us to use our abilities to make ourselves look better.

But knowing Jesus, and knowing that His Spirit gives us different gifts to use for each other, means we'll enjoy being ourselves; that we'll use all that we are to serve His people; and that we'll contentedly let others use their gifts to serve their church—including us, when and where we need it. What a wonderful community that would be!

Incidentally, this is the kind of comparison that it's helpful to teach children, in our churches and in our families. Most schools encourage competition; most children know exactly where they rank against their peers on all kind of measures: multiplication tables, style of shoes, exam results, cell phones and so on.

If you have children, it's just as key for them to know Jesus, and know that eternal blessing comes from knowing Him, as it is for you. Then in their day-to-day lives they're able to praise God for the gifts He's given others, and pray that they will use their own gifts for Him (not, as schools tend to suggest, for furthering their own ambitions and careers). They're able to help those who have "less" in some way than they do. And they're able to live in their world, surrounded by CCS, without feeling pride or envy, but simply experiencing joy in knowing Jesus and the significance, satisfaction and security He gives.

This isn't easy to explain to a child (I've tried)—but that's a subject for another, as yet unwritten, book! The big point is that CCS is no less a danger for children than for adults, and the treatment is just the same—to know, and love knowing, Jesus.

Christians compared with non-Christians

Asaph was a man who followed God about 3,000 years ago, and who experienced a serious bout of looking-up CCS with those around him who didn't know God. When it came to following God, he says, "my feet had almost slipped; I had nearly lost my foothold" (Psalm 73 v 2). He was about to give up. Why? Because:

> *3 I envied the arrogant when I saw the prosperity of the wicked. 4 They have no struggles; their bodies are healthy and strong.*
> *5 They are free from common human burdens … 12 this is what the wicked are like—always free of care, they go on amassing wealth. 13 Surely in vain I have kept my heart pure… 14 Every morning brings new punishments.*
> (Psalm 73 v 3-5, 12-13, 14)

If you're a Christian, can you sympathise with Asaph? Have you ever thought: "Wow, this Christian life is hard work, without much to show for it. And look at that non-Christian friend. She's living for herself, she laughs at the idea of God, and she's doing really well. They've got more money than us. They're healthy, and we're struggling. Life just falls into place for them. I'd love their life. Why do I bother living for God?"

When we find ourselves tempted by a bout of CCS, we need to do what Asaph did:

> *17 I entered the sanctuary of God; then I understood their final destiny. 18 Surely you place them on slippery ground; you cast them down to ruin.* (Psalm 73 v 17-18)

The "sanctuary of God" was the part of the temple where, in Old Testament times, God dwelled among His people. Essentially, Asaph began to look at the world from God's point of view; with an eternal perspective. He took account of the future, of "final destiny". And he realised that all that wealth, health and comfort was built on quicksand. Those who didn't know God were headed for a life beyond death without anything good at all, an existence outside God's love and care. He would "cast them down to ruin".

Understanding the future—our final destination—is key to defeating CCS. What matters is not the journey, but the final destination. Having a first-class ticket is of no use if you're on a trip to nowhere. It's tragic, but it's true, that people who don't acknowledge Jesus as their Creator and Saviour are headed for ruin; for nothing; for eternal misery. However great their life may look now, there is nothing to envy.

In reality, Asaph realises, he is in a far better position, because he knows that one day, God "will take me into glory" (v 24). His glorious destination is secure, because God has secured it. And on the way, though he may sometimes feel like hold luggage, kicked around by life, in fact:

> [23] *I am always with you; you hold me by my right hand.*
> [24] *You guide me with your counsel …* [25] *Whom have I in*
> *heaven but you? And earth has nothing I desire besides you.*
>
> *(Psalm 73 v 23-25)*

Asaph began his psalm with a severe case of CCS as he looked up at non-believers around him. He finishes it content; knowing the blessing of a secure and glorious future, and the satisfaction of knowing God in the here and now. He knows that in God he has everything he will ever need.

The gospel defeats looking-up comparison with non-Christians by reminding us that in Jesus, we already have everything we will ever need.

And it also defeats looking-down comparison with non-Christians. Let's be honest, it's easy to feel that we're better than non-Christians. We live as God wants, at least some of the time; we don't commit what we think of as really bad sins: sleeping around, smoking drugs, skipping church. We had the sense to invite Jesus to be our Saviour as well as our Creator, so that we can enjoy the blessings of knowing Him eternally. Aren't we just, well, a little better, a little wiser than non-Christians around us, who are still seeking blessing in the wrong places?

> *Here is a trustworthy saying, that deserves full acceptance:*
> *Christ Jesus came into the world to save sinners—of whom I*
> *am the worst.* (1 Timothy 1 v 15)

These are Paul's words: a man hand-picked by Jesus to be an apostle, who wrote lots of the New Testament, and who gave up everything to tell others that, in Jesus, they could find all they would ever need.

Yet he still describes himself as "the worst of sinners". Paul knew his heart: that despite knowing Jesus, he naturally put himself at the centre of his life, and looked for blessing elsewhere. And Paul knew the gospel: that it was only through Jesus' death and resurrection, and not through any of his own efforts or achievements, that he had every blessing for eternity.

He knew that it took no less than the death of the Son of God to save him, just as it would take no less than the death of the Son of God to save anyone and everyone else. There was no reason and no excuse for him to look down on anyone. As an eighteenth century-pastor, William Law, once wrote:

> *"We know more of the folly of our own heart than we do*
> *of other people's … [so everyone] may justly look upon*
> *himself to be the greatest sinner that he knows."*

The gospel defeats looking-down comparisons with non-Christians by reminding us that it's only in Jesus, and not in our own performance, that we have everything we will ever need. It frees us from CCS. It gives us contentment.

My relationship with myself

How do I know how I'm doing in life? CCS tells me to compare myself with others to see if I'm doing well enough. But the Bible tells us:

> *[4] Each one should test their own actions. Then they can take*
> *pride in themselves alone, without comparing themselves to*
> *someone else, [5] for each one should carry their own load.*
>
> *(Galatians 6 v 4-5)*

Timothy Keller puts it like this:

> *"God has given each of us a different set of difficulties and*
> *opportunities, a different set of weaknesses and gifts. These*
> *are our 'load'—our responsibility before God."[3]*

So instead of comparing ourselves to "someone else", to whom God has given a different "load" of abilities and circumstances, we need to compare ourselves to… ourselves, to who we could have been for God, given the abilities and circumstances He's given us.

When we stand before God after we die, He's not going to ask us why we didn't have someone else's load; He's going to ask us what we did with ours. We'll have to answer for how we used our life, not someone else's.

So it's useful to ask ourselves: Given the particular load God has given me to carry today, have I acted for Him in all the ways I could have done? How does my day compare to the day I could have had?

This is liberating. We're often very good at looking at others who seem to have a lighter load, and despairing that we're not like them, or becoming bitter with God because He hasn't made us like them. But wonderfully, knowing Jesus is all we need; and Jesus only asks us to live for Him in the situation He has given us.

It's also very challenging, of course. We're often very good at looking at others and feeling proud that we're doing more for God than them, and feeling entitled to extra blessing from God because we're doing better than them, and ignoring the fact that they may be carrying an unseen heavier load. But Jesus is all we need to be blessed, not doing more for Him. And Jesus has simply asked us to live for Him in the situation He has given us.

That's a hard lesson to learn. Even one of Jesus' closest friends during His time on earth took a while to get his head round it. After Jesus had risen, and before He went back to heaven, He took the disciples Peter and John for a walk; and He told Peter that he would be a leader in the church, and that Peter would die by being crucified.

How did Peter respond? He looked at John and said: "Lord, what about him?" (John 21 v 21). He wanted to compare Jesus' plan for his life with Jesus' plan for John's. Who knows whether Peter wanted to check that he would have a higher position in church leadership than John, or whether he would have a worse death than John; whether he was seeking to do looking-down comparison, or anxious about looking-up comparison? But Jesus' reply is short and so, so helpful:

> *If I want him [John] to remain alive until I return, what is*
> *that to you? You must follow me.* (John 21 v 22)

Jesus doesn't want His followers to compare their path through life with others'. He wants them to focus on walking their own. We're to compare ourselves with who we could have been and what we could have done each day; not with who someone else has been or done that day.

There will be times when we can honestly be pleased with how we have carried our particular load. And there will be (many more!) times when we'll know that we could and should have served Jesus more effectively, followed Him more obediently, lived for Him more radically than we have done— and we'll need to ask for forgiveness.

This self-comparison does come with a health warning, though—because we need to guard against this kind of useful self-assessment becoming a trigger for CCS. We can be proud or despairing as we compare ourselves with who God had given us the opportunity to be, just as much as when we compare ourselves with who others are.

But again, the truth that in Jesus we already have all we need frees us from CCS. We need to daily remind ourselves that "it is by grace you have been saved, through faith … not by works, so that no-one can boast" (Ephesians 2 v 8-9). When our works are not what they should have been, there's no need to despair—God in His undeserved kindness, His "grace", has given us all we need in Jesus. And when our works are all that they could have been, that's no cause for boasting, for feeling self-sufficient and entitled to blessing—it is only God's undeserved kindness that gives us all we need in Christ.

However our day has gone, we can be content: content because we know Jesus.

THE CONTENTED
WOMAN

There's a woman in the Bible who threatens to trigger my CCS whenever I think about her. She's only mentioned once in Scripture, and I've put the whole description of her below; see how you feel as you read about her.

> [10] A wife of noble character who can find?
>   She is worth far more than rubies.
> [11] Her husband has full confidence in her
>   and lacks nothing of value.
> [12] She brings him good, not harm,
>   all the days of her life.
> [13] She selects wool and flax
>   and works with eager hands.
> [14] She is like the merchant ships,
>   bringing her food from afar.
> [15] She gets up while it is still night;
>   she provides food for her family
>   and portions for her female servants.

16 She considers a field and buys it;
out of her earnings she plants a vineyard.
17 She sets about her work vigorously;
her arms are strong for her tasks.
18 She sees that her trading is profitable,
and her lamp does not go out at night.
19 In her hand she holds the distaff
and grasps the spindle with her fingers.
20 She opens her arms to the poor
and extends her hands to the needy.
21 When it snows, she has no fear for her household;
for all of them are clothed in scarlet.
22 She makes coverings for her bed;
she is clothed in fine linen and purple.
23 Her husband is respected at the city gate,
where he takes his seat among the elders of the land.
24 She makes linen garments and sells them,
and supplies the merchants with sashes.
25 She is clothed with strength and dignity;
she can laugh at the days to come.
26 She speaks with wisdom,
and faithful instruction is on her tongue.
27 She watches over the affairs of her household
and does not eat the bread of idleness.
28 Her children arise and call her blessed;
her husband also, and he praises her:
29 "Many women do noble things,
but you surpass them all."
30 Charm is deceptive, and beauty is fleeting;
but a woman who fears the LORD is to be praised.

> *³¹ Honour her for all that her hands have done,*
> *and let her works bring her praise at the city gate.*
>
> *(Proverbs 31 v 10-31)*

This sister has caused many a bout of CCS in Christian women.

Here is a woman who has the energy to get up while it's dark (v 15); she sews (v 19) and so is able to keep her home looking good on a budget (v 22); she cares for the poor (v 20), she works part time (v 18, 24); she's totally trustworthy (v 11); she's prepared for anything (v 21); she has a husband, and he's always helped and never hindered by her (v 28-29); and she has children too, who love her and respect her (v 28).

It's easy to see this as the blueprint for the godly woman, wife and mother. So we talk about the benefits of using time wisely; we encourage each other in crafts and living on a tight budget; we set up a soup kitchen for the poor; we support women who go back to work part-time; and so on.

But do you feel despair as you compare your home to hers? Or envy at the fact that she has this happy marriage; or that she's able to have children; or that her children treat her so well; or that her business is thriving? Do you feel inferior and a bit useless? I know I do.

And what if you actually managed to live like her? How would you feel if you had the husband and the children, ran her business, and was as respected as she was? Quite proud of the life you'd made for yourself? A bit superior compared to those "many women" your husband says you "surpass" (v 29)?

In the ways we're not like her, CCS prompts us to look up at her. In any ways we are like her, CCS encourages us to look down on everyone else.

But God doesn't include this woman in His word to trigger CCS. He mentions her so He can point us to the wonderful contentment that comes from defeating CCS. This lady is, first and foremost, "a wife of noble character" (v 10), not a wife of noble deeds.

So what does it mean to have a noble character? What motivated that whole list of things in verses 11-29?

Charm is deceptive, and beauty is fleeting; but a woman who fears the Lord is to be praised. (Proverbs 31 v 30)

The most important thing about this lady is that she feared the Lord, which is Proverbs language for having a right recognition and respect for God. She was a woman who let God be God in her life, who kept Him at the centre. A woman who knew that her gifts of charm and beauty and, presumably, energy, business savvy, wisdom, forward planning, budget-balancing, and so on were "deceptive" and "fleeting"; that they were not what brings true blessing now, nor in the future.

This is a picture of a woman not bogged down in debilitating comparison with others. She's not crippled by the constant sideways glance in the ancient equivalent of shopping centres. She has let God be her God, at the centre of her life; and she is using the circumstances He's given her, and the abilities He's given her, to serve Him. She's content.

So you can follow this woman's example if you are single; if you are young; if you are old; if you are weak; if you are childless; if you are tired or disorganised or poor; if you are unemployed or full-time, housewife, empty-nester or high-flyer.

You can remember that seeking blessing from how you look, what you have or who you are is deceitful and fleeting.

You can find and know and enjoy the blessing you were made to experience: by knowing God, the Lord Jesus, as the centre of your life, and finding that in Him you have all you will ever need.

You can experience real contentment.

CCS is not easy to be rid of. But it is wonderful to live without. This side of death, we'll all be recovering sufferers. But as we live the gospel, letting God be God, treating Jesus as our Creator and Saviour, we can know real blessing. We can experience the significance of being made and loved by Him; and the satisfaction of living for Him; and the security of knowing He will give us fullness of life without end. What a wonderful life He has given us! How can you and I not say…

> *Praise be to the God and Father of our Lord Jesus Christ,*
> *who has blessed us in the heavenly realms with every spiritual*
> *blessing in Christ.*   *(Ephesians 1 v 3)*

That's really the sign of a woman who enjoys a heart which has replaced CCS with contentment: she praises her God, and is looking forward to doing so for ever.

APPENDIX:
WHAT ABOUT...?

We've seen that we don't need to, and shouldn't, be comparing ourselves with others to measure our position or ranking on certain scales. And we've seen that the treatment for this compulsive comparison is treating Christ as our Creator and our Saviour—putting Him at the centre of our universe and finding our significance, satisfaction and security in relating rightly to Him.

But this raises some practical questions:

- *Is it ever right to want to improve my image, circumstances, achievements or "goodness", or should I be content exactly as I am?*
- *Are Christians allowed to be competitive at all, or does it always involve unhealthy comparison?*
- *Is there a place for pride in our accomplishments, or of the accomplishments of those we love, or will this always become an attitude of smug superiority?*

This short section will only start to answer these three questions, but they are questions well worth thinking through in more detail, and discussing further with friends.

1. What about change?

Does all this mean I shouldn't want to change in any way? To improve my appearance, move to a bigger home, get fitter, learn some new skills, pursue a better income, find a boyfriend, have more children, have more obedient children? Is it a case of thinking: "God made me who I am; He's given me my situation, so I have to like it or lump it"? A sort of Christianised version of: "Que sera, sera; whatever will be, will be"?

The answer is yes… and no!

Yes, the fruit of knowing that Christ is at the centre of the universe, and that only He gives us true significance, satisfaction and security, should be contentment—a state of not needing to rail against our situation. We can and should be content in God's goodness and sovereignty. We are not merely resentfully resigned to the status quo, but instead know that our Lord is the only sure place in which to put our trust, whatever our circumstances.

That said, we also know that God doesn't actually want us to remain as we are. He is in the business of change—He longs to transform us. In what sense, and why?

It is not worldly, temporary improvements God is after; it is deep and lasting change—change that sees us become "conformed to the image of his Son" (Romans 8 v 29). God wants us to grow in our character, and in our view of and use of the gifts He's given us, and He wants us to be motivated not by self-protection or self-promotion, but by a desire to display and glorify Christ. Motivation matters to God. So the change itself is not the important thing; the motivation for the change is.

I'm someone who struggles rather a lot with organisation and order, and countless times I've felt like a complete failure when I visit a friend's immaculate house or have been on the receiving end of their impressive administrative capabilities. I often feel as if I am drowning in chaos, and that I am ineffective compared with others, and I want to change. I desperately want to change. But why?

I've come to realise that the motivation is often a desire for others to think better of me, to be impressed by me rather than looking down on me (not that I know that they do—I just tell myself that they do!). But God does not want me to change, even if it's outwardly for the better, if my motive is desire for a higher position on my man-made comparison measures. So I need to purify my heart and seek improvement that means becoming more like Christ, for His glory and not my own.

This means there are times when I need to knuckle down, even though I'm exhausted, to those jobs I hate doing, if that means I am better able to serve others out of love. But at other times, that striving can prove counter-productive to loving others, because it results in high stress. Then I need to accept the chaos and mess, focus on people and their needs, and not worry about what image I am projecting. I need to remember to keep God and His gospel at the centre of my motivations for order, and not myself in competition with others.

There's a traditional prayer which goes like this:

> *"Lord, give me the courage to change the things I can; the serenity to accept the things I can't; and the wisdom to know the difference."*

It's a good thing to ask for—but I think it's most useful if we make a couple of additions: "Lord, give me the courage to change the things I can (and should change); the serenity to accept the things I can't (or shouldn't be so bothered with); and the wisdom to know the difference."

I think this will mean different things to different people. Some may choose to have an image makeover, go on an adult education course, join a Christian internet-dating service, or do home renovation; and they may do those things out of a desire to be less self-conscious and more able to focus on others, or to be able to earn more income in the face of financial stress (or even to give more), or reach out to people with the gospel, or to be in a position to meet a potential spouse without having to leave their current church, or to make hospitality easier. Another woman may do exactly the same things out of a wrong desire— to feel more secure in her looks, or to sound more intelligent in company, or because she feels she'll never be satisfied without a husband, or because she "knows" truly successful women have a beautiful home. The decision and action may be the same; it's the motivation that matters.

2. What about competition?

Are Christians allowed to be competitive? What about those explosive games played on church weekends away? What about Christians involved in professional sport? What about school tennis, debating or tiddlywinks championships? Or submitting your resumé to be a big company along with hundreds of others, all vying for a highly sought-after trainee position? Isn't the aim of all of these to come out "on top", to be the best compared to the opposition?

Competition can be good in many areas of life where it encourages excellence and efficiency rather than mediocrity or sloppiness. It provides goals to work towards. It helps employers in assessing who the best candidate is for the particular role. Competition can even foster unity; a striving against each other but towards the same goal, such as the team members who compete against one another in training so they can spur one another on to improve their game and increase the chances of the whole team winning.

Alex Chediak has some helpful insights in his article, *Christians and Competition*, in Boundless Webzine (boundless. org/2005/articles/a0001572.cfm):

> *"Assigning merit-based grades and letting the best team or player win encourages excellence and helps individuals discern their strengths. Whether we redouble our efforts in an area of weakness, or re-channel them into an area of greater personal aptitude, the recognition of excellence leads to improvements in performance—and not just for the winning party."*

And this is what Stuart Weir says in *What the Book says about Sport*:

> *"Sport lives by comparison. Although many claim that they compete to find their own limits of performance, this can only be established by comparison with others' performance. To be better than someone else is a basic thought in sport. We need competition in order to judge our own performance.*
> *The literal meaning of 'compete' is to strive together ... Christian competition is about striving with all our*

> *might but within the rules and etiquette of the game. It is striving to maximise the gifts God has given us in a competitive environment. Will not the God who promised us 'life ... to the full' (John 10 v 10) rejoice when we compete and reach our full potential?" (page 69)*

The challenge for Christians is to check our motives as we enter a competitive arena of any sort. Am I taking part in the competition to raise my position among my peers in order to boost my sense of significance, or am I taking part to grow and reach my full potential in that particular skill, in God's strength, for His glory? Or in the case of "fun" competition (like playing a board game with the family), is my aim to help grow relationships and openness as we battle it out together, rather than to impress people and gain their admiration?

It's helpful to view others, especially other Christians, as running mates rather than rivals. Christ, not me, is at the centre of all things; significance, satisfaction and security are found through being in right relationship with my Creator. Others are not the enemy, the obstacle to my "success" in life. It is not a case of survival of the fittest. I do not need to beat them to be blessed.

If we're parents, it'll help our children if we teach and model to them from an early age that their identity is secure in knowing they're made by God, and loved by Him in Christ Jesus, so they don't need to seek approval or significance by being better than others. They are free to be competitive in certain contexts, if it is for the sake of doing their best, seeking to improve their skills and rejoicing in the abilities God has given them. But a competitive attitude must involve perseverance, endurance and grace rather than irritation, rudeness, anger, arrogance or despondency. Quite a challenge for adults as well as children, I know!

3. What about being proud?

"I'm so proud of you," we might tell a friend who's picked themselves up after a difficult experience, or made a good decision despite it making their life more difficult. "I'm so proud of you," we tell our husband as they get a well-deserved promotion or complete their first DIY project! "I'm so proud of you," we tell our children when their team has come first in the relay race at sports day, or when they've shone in their music performance at the school concert, or learned to share with one of their little friends.

Is that right? Is there a place for being proud of those we love, or even proud of our own performance?

Again, no, and yes, because the question is: what are we proud of? The superior position, the reflected glory that comes to us? Or the effort, or the outcome? To put it another way, does our pride result in us praising ourselves in some way, or praising God for enabling the effort and working the outcome?

In this sense, our pride in a loved one's achievements should actually be a sense of gratitude to God for enabling their efforts, and enabling us to help, so that they are able to do the right thing, bounce back from failing, make a costly decision, and so on. It shouldn't be them "winning" or being "one of the best" that determines our praise and pride, but their perseverance in some challenge, and humility as they achieve—or fail.

Sophie de Witt

The same applies to Christian discipling. Graham Beynon (in *Mirror, Mirror,* page 114—see "Useful books to read" on page 107) points us to an example of Paul's "pride" in his ministry among the Thessalonian church: "For what is our hope, our joy, or the crown in which we will glory in the presence of our Lord Jesus when he comes? Is it not you? Indeed, you are our glory and joy" (1 Thessalonians 2 v 19-20).

> "Paul says he will 'glory' in these people— that is what has been achieved in them. They are his crown! He's not embarrassed about what he's achieved, is he? But Paul has previously thanked God for how these people became Christians and have grown as Christians (see 1 Thessalonians 1 v 2-3; 2 v 13). Why? Because God is the one at work in them through Paul.
> So how should Paul feel about all he has achieved? Could I suggest 'humble dignity'? Paul can have a great feeling of dignity, even pride, at what he has done, but it is humble because it was only because of God working through him."

There's nothing wrong with having and sharing a sense of blessing, privilege or wonder at a friend or family member's development, or the Christian growth of someone you have been praying for and encouraging. What is wrong is to root our pride in ourselves, or someone we know, doing better than others, so that they or we get glory and praise.

The success of someone we love (including ourselves!) is a trigger for CCS-based pride. It's also an opportunity for God-praising, grateful pride. As I said in chapter six, we need to make each Compulsive Comparison trigger-event a fresh

102

opportunity to go back to the Lord and wrestle through our hopes and dreams, our identity and worth, with Him; an opportunity once again to put Christ at the very centre and to experience His peace.

ENDNOTES

[1] Annie Sanders, *Warnings and Gales,* page 411 (published Orion)

[2] Timothy Keller, *Counterfeit Gods,* page xix (Penguin)

[3] Timothy Keller, *Galatians For You,* page 153 (The Good Book Company)

USEFUL BOOKS

On exploring the Christian faith

One Life: What's It All About? Rico Tice & Barry Cooper

Original Jesus, Carl Laferton

Prodigal God, Timothy Keller

If You Could Ask God One Question,
Paul Williams & Barry Cooper

Books for women

*Calm My Anxious Heart: A Woman's Guide to Finding
Contentment,* Linda Dillow

Lies Women Believe, Nancy Leigh DeMoss

What women really want need, Lesley Ramsey

On idolatry and identity

Counterfeit Gods, Timothy Keller

Idols, Julian Hardyman

Mirror, Mirror, Graham Beynon

On keeping God in the centre

Desiring God and *Future Grace,* John Piper

Helpful group Bible studies

The Good Book Guide to Contentment, Anne Woodcock

The Good Book Guide to Biblical Womanhood, Sarah Young

THANK YOU...

...to Rebekah Brown, for first asking me to speak on the subject at the KZN Women's Convention in South Africa in 2010, and helping me think through and structure the material in the run up to the event.

...to the 70+ people who completed my survey on CCS; and to all the people who shared your stories, and whose words I've quoted in this book (you know who you are!).

...to the dear friends with whom I have chatted in depth about the subject, and those who read through various drafts of the book: Sydnie J, Sarie K, Ali S, Heather J, Taryn H, Laura D, Sue H, Jane V, Sue & Debbie dW, Cathy F, Rico T, Lizzie L, Claire R, and Mum! Thanks for your time and wisdom.

...to John Piper of Desiring God, whose varied and repeated appeals to treasure Christ above all and so give more glory to God have been hugely influential in the growth of my faith over the last decade or so.

...to my editor, Carl Laferton, at The Good Book Company, who has become more of a partner in the ministry of this book than simply an editor. Thank you for your huge encouragement flowing from personal excitement about this topic, as well as your invaluable feedback, insightful ideas... and even your cutting!

...to my husband Chris, who is a true gift of God's grace. Thank you for allowing me to take on this project, which has often been carried out to your detriment. Thank you for being my best possible partner and leader in gospel ministry and in life.

As women, we are often encouraged to "count our blessings". But truly biblical gratitude is much more than this. Mary K. Mohler helps us grow in gracious gratitude (thanking God for who he is) as well as natural gratitude (thanking him for his blessings)—and deals with some of the things that hinder us. Read this to rediscover the joy of a thankful heart.

"I want the heart of this book to seep into my own."
Rosaria Butterfield

thegoodbook.co.uk | .com / gig

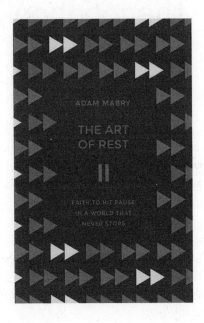

ADAM MABRY

THE ART
OF REST

FAITH TO HIT PAUSE
IN A WORLD THAT
NEVER STOPS

For some of us, resting seems like a waste of time—it means we're missing out on other things. For others, rest seems like a luxury—there's simply too much to do. And almost all of us crave refreshing rest at times—but find we're not sure how to actually do it. This warm, realistic, humorous book shows us the huge spiritual and emotional rewards of real Christian rest.

"This little jewel of a book made my heart sing."
Clare Heath-Whyte

thegoodbook.co.uk | .com / rest

thegoodbook
COMPANY

BIBLICAL | RELEVANT | ACCESSIBLE

At The Good Book Company, we are dedicated to helping Christians and local churches grow. We believe that God's growth process always starts with hearing clearly what he has said to us through his timeless word—the Bible.

Ever since we opened our doors in 1991, we have been striving to produce Bible-based resources that bring glory to God. We have grown to become an international provider of user-friendly resources to the Christian community, with believers of all backgrounds and denominations using our books, Bible studies, devotionals, evangelistic resources, and DVD-based courses.

We want to equip ordinary Christians to live for Christ day by day, and churches to grow in their knowledge of God, their love for one another, and the effectiveness of their outreach.

Call us for a discussion of your needs or visit one of our local websites for more information on the resources and services we provide.

Your friends at The Good Book Company

thegoodbook.com | thegoodbook.co.uk
thegoodbook.com.au | thegoodbook.co.nz
thegoodbook.co.in